TRANSITION NOW

First published in 2010 by
Red Wheel/Weiser, LLC
With offices at:
500 Third Street, Suite 230
San Francisco, CA 94107
www.redwheelweiser.com

ISBN: 978-1-57863-474-3
Library of Congress Cataloging-in-Publication Data is available upon request.

Cover and text design by Tracy Johnson
Typeset in Garamond 3 and Trade Gothic Condensed
Cover photograph © 2008 Christine Glade

Printed in Canada
TCP
10 9 8 7 6 5 4 3 2 1
The paper used in this publication meets the minimum requirements of the American National Standard for Information Sciences—Permanence of Paper for Printed Library Materials Z39.48-1992 (R1997).

TRANSITION NOW

REDEFINING DUALITY • 2012 AND BEYOND

featuring Lee Carroll & Kryon,
Patricia Cori & The Sirian High Council,
and Pepper Lewis & Gaia

edited by Martine Vallée

CONTENTS

Introduction: Our World, Our Choice

Here I am again ... greeting you as you are about to start reading the second book in the series Toward 2012. For my French readership, it is the fourth book since it all started in 2007. I am simply amazed and grateful to see the unfolding of this series. My only wish has always been that those who feel an affinity for these teachings be able to read them.

Again, a very special thank you to everyone at Weiser Books, particularly to Jan Johnson for deciding that this book is worth the while. Publishers have so many possibilities to choose from, so many great authors to publish, that choosing this work is really a conscious decision on their part and an honor on mine. Special thanks also to my agent, Luc Jutras, for making all this seem so easy.

And thanks to you, the reader; even though my work is mainly in the written word, there are really no words to say how grateful I am that so many of you have chosen to read *The Great Shift* and seem to have enjoyed it. So here we are once more, meeting through the written word for *Transition Now: Redefining Duality, 2012 and Beyond.*

My guests for this installment are Lee Carroll/Kryon, followed by Patricia Cori/The Sirian High Council, and then Pepper Lewis/Gaia.

Lee Carroll and Kryon are the only pair that has been part of this series since the beginning and will be until the end. Why? Simply because they are a major influence on the spiritual lives of so many people. The information they share is such a great combination of science, spirituality, consciousness, and compassion that I feel every aspect of our spiritual lives can be touched by these writings. Like no other, Kryon has shown me not only how we are the great creator of our lives but what it means to go beyond the third dimension. I really do think Lee Carroll is one of the most interesting speakers on the circuit right now, so the combination of the two—well, it's pretty amazing.

Patricia Cori and the Sirian High Council are another powerful combination. Patricia is such a wonderful lady—a woman with a big heart and a great mission and completely devoted to it. The Sirians have been so important for our Earth evolution that I decided that Patricia should be part of this project once again. Furthermore, she brings groups to sacred sites all over the world. I went to Egypt with her in January 2009, and it was outstanding. One powerful moment was a meditation that we did at the beginning of our trip—I can say without a doubt that it was the most powerful meditation I have ever done. So powerful was it that I asked the High Council what happened during the meditation. You will have their input in Patricia's section.

Pepper Lewis and Gaia offer a new perspective in this series. For a while now, I have been looking pretty closely at Pepper's work. Last year, in the French edition, I included one of her articles about the disappearance of the bees from this planet. Previously, it had been a mystery to me, while everyone gave a unique version—from the scientific community to beekeepers to *60 Minutes*. Then I read what Gaia had to say, and it seems to be the most credible information on the subject that I have read anywhere. Who better than Gaia to tell us about what is happening in nature? So I ask her to share some pretty interesting information.

Each time I start a book, I first ask myself: What do I feel inside? What am I living? Then I try to develop different aspects of that energy to better understand it and also to understand how it relates to the world. That's where my questions come from and where my intuition guides me.

Now I feel we are entering another phase... a powerful transition. This transition started with us, but our children and grandchildren will complete the greatest transition that the human race has ever known. I really do think that the success of this transition will depend on our capacity as individuals and world citizens to firmly put into action the new basis of evolution—and that means becoming conscious of our choices, of our world. It is one thing to read about consciousness and quite another to live consciously.

From my point of view, we human beings are at our best when we are engaged together in the act of transforming the world, not only in concentrating on our individual transformation. Many times I have seen firsthand what happens when individuals are aligned on a quest—the collective intelligence often produces powerful results, much more than with just any individual.

There is no doubt that we are going toward a higher consciousness at an accelerated rate; and every time we make a gesture toward that goal, the process is even more accelerated. One great example of this is the presidential election of

Barak Obama. This was not just the election of a new president, but it was in fact the election of a higher consciousness—one that created hope everywhere on the planet. Hope that it is possible for things to change for the better.

I realized the collective feeling about this election one evening when I was watching the news on a Canadian channel. The broadcast was presenting the reaction of people everywhere in the world, from Japan to Germany, from France to Brazil. But one place stayed in my mind: Africa. It showed a group of three people together in a very small village. They had no shoes; their clothes were, well... a little bit torn, a little bit dirty, but they all had these big smiles on their faces and were holding a sign that read: *We trust you*. To me it felt more like: *Now we have hope for us too*. In that moment, I realized that this election was much more than an American event; it was a worldwide event. The fact that people from a small village in Africa felt a concern for what was happening in America told me that, even without knowing each other, we all felt something special was happening—and we all wanted to say so. You chose to do this, you elected this man who, for many, represents a higher way of doing things. In doing so, you elevated the consciousness of a planet and gave hope to an entire humanity... not an easy thing to do these days. Hopefully, other countries will follow. You will read what Kryon has to say about it.

One last fascinating note about your president: According to Richard Lederer, a master of anagram and riddle, when you scramble the letters together of Barak Hussein Obama, you obtain: *Abraham Is Back, One U.S.* This is quite symbolic, wouldn't you say, considering that Abraham Lincoln is the one who put an end to slavery in 1863? And by now, we all know how Lincoln is a great source of inspiration to Obama. Furthermore, both men were lawyers and both started their political careers in the state of Illinois!

But if we look beyond the warm persona of this president and the challenges before him, it is very clear now that people, as members of this humanity, demand leaders who bear the image of this consciousness that is rising and that we all feel. *Yes, we can*—the famous quote we heard in almost every speech he gave—was, in my opinion, an arrow of intention directed toward the consciousness of each individual. These three words represent not only the grace of what real consciousness is all about but also confidence in the power of transformation.

Dear friends, I leave you with these few words. Everyone on this planet is part of the transformation that is happening. Consciously or not, we all know that we are part of an unparalleled event: *the transformation of the human race*. It is our journey together as a group called *humanity* rather than an individual journey as a person called *me*.

As part of this transformation, we need to work toward the goal of enforcing the right of all people to be free and to express themselves without the fear of being killed, raped, or tortured. All people on this planet have the right to live with a roof over their heads, to feed their families, to receive medical assistance when they are sick or injured, and to find God any way they choose. But if we let others decide what we should do with our consciousness—the heart of our being—then we will never be free. We have to be the leaders of our own life and to treat each other with dignity and respect. Then we will be able to find our common destiny. That is what this great experiment is all about, and it is remarkable and unique.

Finally, readers, even though I may not have had the chance to meet you in person, I think of you often, knowing that no matter which countries we come from, we are all traveling together with the same purpose and determination. Uniting in conscious thought toward a global renaissance is much more powerful than being physically together with people who have no inspiration or global engagement.

I know in my heart that there is a collective force being born right at this moment… and it is the beginning of the greatest transition ever.

Take care of yourself, take care of the ones you love, and let's take care of each other.

—*Martine Vallée*
JULY 2009
MONTREAL, CANADA

PART ONE

KRYON

Introduction by Lee Carroll

The book you hold in your hands is yet another in the very successful series of books created by Martine Vallée. This book contains more esoteric information than ever. The Earth is obviously moving in a way that reveals the shift currently in process. Mainstream media, as well as people who are spiritual, are beginning to notice. Even the planet is reeling under what has happened in the last U.S. election. "They did something right!" they are saying. Something happened!

How do the coming years differ from those in the recent past? It is now getting harder to measure spirituality and growth. This is due to the fact that we are starting to tap interdimensional energies in a 3-D world. The only way to move forward is to study what is expected by Spirit—start melding your mind into another reality that allows for things felt but unseen.

When entire governments begin to shift, you know something is up. When you chase greed out of an economy, it's like chasing blood out of the human body. Some say it's built into the entire system, but that happened along the way. At the risk of killing the entire system, the economy of the United States is being pruned. The transfusion of new blood will take a while, and hopefully the patient will not die (it won't). But this is the analogy of the kinds of change we are seeing. All this since the last book!

Join Martine as she again selects the energies and authors that will help to clarify what is happening and keep up with the shift that we are all feeling so profoundly. Things are changing quickly. Perhaps this is the best and most current guide you can have to know more about it all.

—*Lee Carroll*

From Kryon

Greetings, dear ones. I am Kryon from magnetic service.

The next stage is upon you. Going through the shift will require a transition of energy that we have just begun speaking about. You might think that the shift is something that is happening to the Earth, governments, weather, and economies, but the fact is that the shift is for *you*, and it is *you* who it affects the most. The shift is the "decision point" many have spoken about that can change the future of the planet. In the process, humans are asked to wake up to the potentials of changing the very DNA that is the core of their akash and the creator of change at a quantum level. So becoming quantum is the task at hand, and it requires a rethinking of everything that used to be on your linear time line.

What is it you are here for? Are you indeed stuck with what you see in the mirror? Can you control the body's aging process? Can you thwart disease and ill health? Everything I have listed is far more understandable at a quantum level... the very attribute of over 90 percent of your DNA's chemistry, for within the DNA loop there is only 4 percent that is linear. The rest of the chemistry represents the quantum instruction sets that are now being activated by the shift before you. Seemingly random, this chemical signature has been the antenna for change on this planet—and a specifically profound change within the human body. Your DNA is sacred, and much of it is viewable in a linear way but only understandable in a quantum way. Over 90 percent of the chemistry is ready to receive new instructions!

As the grid shifts, and the magnetic energy of the planet becomes less, not only do you see changes in the weather but consciousness is also changing, and you are seeing that as well. Rather than being a simple observer, you now have the ability to reap the benefits of this very shift you created back in 1987. The time is right, and the information is coming from many intuitives all over the Earth. DNA is awakening to higher potentials, and the gifts of Spirit are beginning to show themselves.

Is it possible to have peace over all this? Can you begin to slow down your biological clock, eliminate what you thought were permanent blocks in your life, and become healthier than you were in your youth? This is the promise of Spirit and the information that we have been giving you for almost twenty years. The majority of your DNA is quantum, yet you have been linear for eons. It's time to begin to activate the chemistry that has lain there dormant for all this time. This is what the shift is for!

Blessed is the human who takes this book seriously, and not just as a passing reading experience. Consider much of the information here as the beginning of a profound change in humanity.

And so it is.

—*Kryon*

ONE

OUR HOLOGRAPHIC NATURE

I think that the next big thing for all of us to understand is our holographic nature. A hologram is above all gathered information, but what is fascinating to me is that if we take a hologram and cut it in pieces, we still have the same information embedded in one small piece. We can divide it into minuscule pieces if we choose, but it is still all there. Just as the whole is held within the part. So because we are a piece of the Universe, that would mean that we can also access all the information embedded in the Universe.

I know that my input of what is a hologram is probably pretty basic, and the complexity of it is probably much more complicated, but is it somewhat accurate?

Greetings, dear one.

We again are here at your request to give you answers that are delivered through my human partner of twenty years. We give them in love, as best we can through this deep veil of dimensional differences.

You ask if your above statement is somewhat accurate. The answer is that it is as accurate as you can conceive, being in the dimension you are. Your quantum hologram is defined as the part of God you carry on Earth, but it can't be truly understood and shouldn't be. Instead, it is to be acknowledged and used the best you can within your 3-D experience.

You are very quickly reaching that situation in which a true understanding of what the new energy is bringing you really cannot be achieved. We are aware of the human mind's tendency to believe it can think about anything, but it truly is limited to the dimensionality it believes it is in. So think as you might on high thoughts, you still can't conceive of the things you can't conceive of. Yet you are asked to use these things you can't conceive of and to try to make sense of them.

Really, this is no different than how you use many technical devices that you don't fully understand. You use your energy freely, but most of you have no idea how it's generated. You see the machines and the facilities, but how many of you truly understand multiphase electricity? This was brought to you by a very high thinker, and he was the only one on the planet to actually think "out of the box" and bring you the concept of multiphase current. This push-pull idea is not linear and needed a conceptual thinker. It has been used ever since, but most of you have no understanding of what it means or how it's produced. This, however, does not stop you from the full use of it. Now you depend on it.

So there has to be awareness of the human hologram, or Higher Self, but Spirit is never going to ask you to understand it all. Instead, we are encouraging everyone who is reading this to acknowledge that it's there and to begin using it. This is harder than you think, for it requires you to trust things like intuition and energies from within yourself that you didn't know you had. This truly is the challenge of Lightworkers in this new age. You must change your own awareness of who you think you are.

Is there something important missing in this statement?

Yes, there is... something very big. Your human hologram includes the "you" parts of you that are on the other side of the veil, designed to interact with a quantum system. You think, even in your ignorance of what the hologram is, that it is still around you here on Earth. In a quantum state, there is no distance or place for anything. It just *is*. Therefore, you are not aware of the part of you that split off when you came to Earth, the portion that still remains on the other side of the veil. This is a very active part of the whole system of *you*, and you are not ready yet to conceive of it.

TWO

GETTING OUT OF THE ILLUSION BY UNDERSTANDING OUR HOLOGRAPHIC NATURE

The physical world that we experience so substantially is a mirage created by the holographic nature of matter. My example of this would be that our consciousness is like a laser beam of coherent light and that we, humanity as a whole, have all chosen to hold the lens of our consciousness so that together we see the same thing through this light.

If that is so, to get out of the illusion of this, we can change the focus of our lens. We do not have to see the same thing the rest of the world sees. These illusions are created and sustained by how we hold our focus of our awareness. But I do not think that this could be done by simply thinking our way out of it. It must come from a profound level of consciousness, in my opinion, and it takes a very special kind of alignment or a very focused intention—or maybe in fact it is the mix of the two... a powerful alignment of awareness.

Kryon, I can understand that we need to do this, but I have trouble seeing clearly how to do it. I would think that the brain and the nervous system would be involved. Do we need to train our nervous system to perceive this altered state of perception?

Yes, you do, and this is very profound insight. It must start with an alteration of thinking based on things unseen and not understood. When some of you started this journey, it was a stretch of the imagination from everything you were told. You had to train your brain and nervous system that there were energies waiting to be felt and that there was a parent energy of God that was not only within you but also outside of you. These two were waiting for a reconnection to take place... one that could only happen with your intent to move past what you thought was reality.

Remember how, when you started to meditate, you felt nothing? Many around you were going to higher levels and coming back with such perception and peace... and you? You didn't get much, and you really didn't want to admit that to anyone. Remember, I know who is reading these words!

After a while, however, you begin to feel the energy of Spirit around you. You are actually training your perception (brain and nervous system) to allow these energies to exist in your reality. You are changing the hologram to include things within your sphere of consciousness that were never there before. So I ask you: What has happened, really? Are these energies new? Did you create them?

The answer is no. They were always there. Therefore, you are in discovery mode every time you meditate and read words like these. Have you ever wondered what else there is that you haven't allowed yourself to feel or discern yet? What about mastery? That's what happens when you begin to let your divinity show.

At this stage, can we even do this? If we could go forward, obviously we could get out of duality.

We should define *getting out of duality* for the sake of this book, because it is the title and the energy of the writings here.

Duality is the dichotomy of energy that you are born with. It is intentional, designed, and represents the core of the test you have all your lives. It represents the dark and light attributes of any human, set upon you by the history of the planet's vibration as created by humans throughout the ages. Duality is appropriate for all of you and has been very stable in its vibratory proportion, but it is starting to take a huge backseat to the reason you are here in this new energy shift. Duality is starting to shift as well, taking on a new proportion of dark to light.

In 1989, we told you about the ability to void your karmic imprint. This was the beginning of getting out of on old duality. Karma is the process of the creation of energy within human life that takes care of unfinished business. It gives you purpose and passion and creates appropriate challenge. All of these things give you opportunities to grow and solve energy puzzles. But this is a very old process and is automatic. It gives the individual human no choice. Many of your very ancient belief systems speak of karma and its purpose in life. It is part of a very ancient system and has been the way of things for many thousands of years.

Enter the new human in a new age when Earth's dynamic hologram is shifting. The Great Shift, as you call it, is a reprogramming of the hologram of the Earth, humans, human nature, and the very future of the planet. Therefore, the system is changing. Make no mistake, karma will always be the beginning energy for every human. Duality is there too, but each one of you has a choice to remove this karma—to move through duality and get on with other things.

I reveal to you that when I first started talking through my partner, we spoke of something called the Implant. My partner told me that this was an inappropriate word and another one should be used. But we used it anyway, on purpose—for it represented permission to implant yourself with the energy of a karma-free human consciousness and a duality that had shifted. This would be profound and should not be entered into lightly. So we started talking about it twenty years ago, and now you know why, for it represents "getting out of the old energy duality."

Duality will always be there, but many of you are learning to void it so completely that it's like an old shoe that sits unused in the corner. It still belongs to you, and occasionally it will make a lot of noise, asking to be worn again, but you have learned that it has no control over you—and you know how to make it quiet down. Most of humanity does not, though, and is actually guided by it or even controlled by it.

So the answer is that indeed you are learning how to void a duality that was created to facilitate your old karmic imprints. Most of humanity is still there with this old energy and may remain there. There is nothing wrong with that, and this is a free choice. But less than 0.5 percent of people, if they void this duality, can create light for the rest of the world. This will affect everything, for when the light is turned on, even those in the old energy get to see what has been hidden for centuries.

Mass human consciousness is this way: not all have to believe what you believe, but you can never put the demon back in the box, so to speak. In other words, once humanity sees a better way, it tends to create its own energy around change. Look at it this way: The lighthouse shines its light, and hundreds of ships change course. None of the ships have to be lighthouses. They depend on the lighthouse to show the way, and with this everything changes and they all steer a better course away from the rocks. One lighthouse, many ships.

Maybe also the Universe needs a place like this to experience evolution. Do you, on the other side, need us in order to experience who you truly are? Is this experience part of creating a new hologram of the Universe?

Again, a sublimely profound expression of your insight has appeared. Is what you do as a human affecting something else grander than you? Could your work here on Earth be the precursor to something that might actually change the Universe? The answer is yes, and I have discussed it with you for over twenty years. What you do here affects everything. If this is the only planet of free choice, have you ever wondered why? Have you ever then projected the possibility that the planet is here for a reason greater than itself?

Let's say that the hologram that is being created is about quantum energy. Let's also say that since it's quantum, you cannot separate the things of the Universe from the things of a divine human being. Therefore, let's say that everything that happens on this planet changes something that you can't conceive of but which is everywhere. Again, there will be those who say, "Well, Kryon, just tell us! Why beat around the subject like this?" When you leave the house and the dog is sad, you could explain to him that you are just going on an errand, list the names of the stores you are going to visit, and say what time you are going to return, but the dog wouldn't have the intellect to understand anything about your errands or how to tell time. All he wants is your energy. When you return, he acts as if you have been gone for years! Such is his intellectual simplicity.

Humans feel that their intellect is as high as it can get. They say, "I am the only animal on the planet who can contemplate his own existence. Therefore, I am unlimited in my ability to think." This simply is not true. You simply represent the highest evolved intellect on the planet, but hardly the highest one possible. This is often your weakness, the idea that you can think your way out of your own intellectual box. You can't any more than the dog could. There was a limit to his process, and you have one too. All around you it is obvious that there are levels of intellect, but to you suddenly your own process isn't included at all in the levels of consciousness. You see it as the top of the top and the highest of the high. But it's simply another level.

When you begin to realize this, you open yourself to the question: how can I accelerate the evolution of my existence and my own process of perception? Then you begin a quantum journey, for the next step in your intellectual pursuits is the one that bridges dimensions.

THREE

OUR CHANGING BRAIN FROM LEFT TO RIGHT

I once read a book called A Whole New Mind *by Daniel H. Pink. It stated that "the right-brainers will rule the world." When I thought about it, I completely agreed with it. We are entering a new era in which right-brain qualities like artistry, empathy, storytelling, meaning, and purpose in what we do will become much more important in our lives. The more linear, logical brain associated with accounting, law, and engineering will be less crucial in the years to come than the right brain will be.*

The conceptual age we are entering is much more our time. For so long, right-brain people were seen as spacey, living in the clouds, like hippies. Many believed it was impossible to make a living when you were right brain. But now we are taken seriously... finally. I see creativity everywhere. I have so many ideas now that I carry a recorder and record all the ideas that I have. They just come pouring out.

Also, these kind of qualities cannot be outsourced. We cannot outsource creativity, passion, or healing qualities because they are unique to each of us. From what I see, many jobs of the left brain are being outsourced to other countries! Many people are losing their jobs.

Many of us don't just want things, we want things that have meaning. We don't just want to have a job, we want a job that we like that brings out the best in us. We don't just want to share our abundance, but we want to share with the right people or organization.

Is this a good picture of what is happening right now with our brains? Is this happening because of the energy, the change in our DNA, etc.? What exactly is causing this? I think our brain is living its own transition.

The best way of seeing how this works is by looking at your own North American scenario. As your culture has developed and matured, it has gone from the left brain to the right brain when it comes to production and trade. There was a time when you made all your own steel, for instance. Now others do it for you. It's the same with almost all the manufacturing. Others now make your clothes, cars, and other things that used to be the staples of your industry. So what do you make now? Intellectual properties. They're the software and the ideas and the research and the items that improve human life. Gone are the manufacturing jobs, and instead the right-brainers have begun to emerge.

This is a macrocosm of what you are saying regarding the microcosm of your internal existence. You are moving to quality instead of quantity, purpose instead of routine, and the pursuit of a reason for living. This is what really sets the old energy apart from the new. You are broaching the interdimensional doorway.

One of the best examples that I've seen of these qualities is the election of Barak Obama in 2008. He is certainly one of the best storytellers that I've seen.

There is so much information available everywhere that now what counts is not only the way we receive information but also how it is delivered and the emotional impact it has on us. From my perspective, Obama's greatest quality was that he built connection, not only in the United States but throughout the world. We felt connected to his dream, and we really thought that we could do it. He was so good at delivering his message that we believed him; he inspired millions of people. He has vision, and now the whole world thinks "Yes, we can" is a powerful message. They are not only words, they are words with meaning, and citizens heard them because they were ready for change.

Kryon, I would like you to talk about the impact of this election not from a third-dimensional view but rather from a multidimensional one. I am sure that it was so powerful that it certainly elevated the consciousness of the planet.

Let us back up a moment. First, let's say that Spirit does not care about your politics. Spirit did not place this man in office; the citizens of the United States did, with total free will. In the process, they violated all the old energy rules of their own culture. Since the United States began, the race issue has prevailed. They fought the Civil War over it, and forty years ago they passed laws against it. Even still, the old ways do not pass away quickly, and they perpetuate from one generation to the next. Ask anyone of color. It's still there.

Something has happened, however, that reflects a mass consciousness—something we actually predicted would occur. There is no other explanation as to how a black man got to be the president of this land. His election was fair and undisputed. Many of the states who were from the Deep South, formerly bastions of prejudice, voted for him. How could this happen? There were those who said it could never happen, yet here it is. What does it mean?

There is a history lesson here about hate and prejudice, and I want to digress even more to make a point about old and new energy. The Middle East issues are an example of thousands of years of a static hatred. Each family teaches its young to hate the ones they hate. The result is that nothing ever changes. One generation dies and another one is born, and they all hate the same ones their parents hated. There is so much hatred that it spills over in the dialogue of the leadership, giving even more reason to hate. It perpetuates itself, and it's seemingly never-ending.

Many of you in America fought a war a half century ago, when the enemy attacked you and started a world war in the Asian Pacific. That enemy was hated too, and there were internment camps for people who looked like them and a great deal of publicity against their race and their country. The hate ran strong, and an entire generation was involved. Ask your parents and grandparents how these people were spoken of and how they were seen. It was ugly.

Yet all of this changed, seemingly overnight. Now Japan is allied with you so much that if either of your economies fail, so does the other. The Japanese are part of your culture now, and you can't do without them. They are no longer enemies but instead highly respected friends. Travel is common between you, and you exchange energies of trade and commerce as if nothing ever happened! That was only two generations ago. What happened to allow this?

The answer is that when Japan was defeated and the war machine was eliminated in that country, the Japanese didn't resent you. Their culture is one of harmony, and it began to create an understanding between you. They didn't perpetuate hate as a conquered country. This respect was returned by you. You couldn't help it, because their light showed the way.

You didn't teach your children to hate them either. Think of it! Do you see how the hate chain was broken? All it took was someone to step forward and create the consciousness that wouldn't keep the hatred going. This is new energy thinking, and you saw it first with this situation.

Now, let's return to the U.S. election: it could never have happened unless there was a consciousness shift in the culture of your country. Indeed, people listened to inspiring words, but this wasn't the reason Obama won the vote. He is black, and no matter what his words were, in the past millions were taught not to trust a man such as he. But they did.

You are seeing proof of the shift upon you—things that could not happen in the past are beginning to happen. Look for proof of your own consciousness evolution within these things! It's beginning to happen.

Now, for those of you who want some insight as to who Obama might be, I give you only a couple of things to ponder. First, it is of no consequence what other universal dimension he is from. This has no bearing at all on anything, for all of you are pieces of God who come from energies that you can't even imagine. You call them places and give them credibility, but most of you can't imagine the reality of how it works. Let it go, for it's a nonissue.

What is an issue is his Earth history. This man has Indigo qualities. He is an old, original Indigo and was identified as such more than four years ago when he gave his first national speech at the convention where most of the world got to see him. The savant Nancy Tappe, who has the sight of a synesthetic and who first identified the indigo color of consciousness, made this admission to those around her at the time. It is now published as *Understanding Your Life Through Color*.

This begins to explain some of Obama's attributes, for look at the criticisms during his campaign to gain this leadership seat. Those who opposed him said he had no experience at all! Yet when you saw him, he seemed to act and speak as if he had much experience. There was something about him that said to you: "Inside, he has had all the experience needed." This is the classic Indigo. They feel they have been there many times; the lack of actual third-dimensional historic experience doesn't seem to bother them. This is why there is so much trouble with Indigo young people at the moment who are now entering the workplace. They don't want to start at the bottom! They act like they have had all the experience they need to be promoted right away.

Here is a hint about Obama's akash. He was born in pure Lemurian energy. Hawaii is the place where Lemuria started and ended. It is no accident. You are looking at an old Lemurian leader who has the consciousness of the new breed of human now coming into the planet. Suddenly you have an Indigo as president of the United States, and how long did you think that would take? We told you about that possibility in a channeling a few years before. It was a strong potential.

Finally, the unspoken attribute. He is not black. He is a combination of a white and black union—something even more shocking to many in the old energy. The marriage of his parents was actually illegal in their state when they united. You see what we are telling you? Obama not only represents a new kind of conceptual thinking, but he also represents the idea of cultures and races coming together to create a human who is not an outcast at all but rather the beginning of the new kind of human: a meld of races and ideas, one who never takes sides because he represents both of them.

What is it like for a man to receive so much love from millions of people? How does this love impact his energy body?

He is used to it. His akash reeks with it, and he has been there before. Therefore, his hologram is one that fully understands this position and will not abuse it unless he slips back into duality, which is his choice. But Indigos don't do that. Their consciousness is one of great independence and conceptual thinking. A conceptual thinker is one who is above the linearity of the old ways. They don't even see them.

Obama's greatest threat will be from those who hate his optimism and his integrity. There are those who wish to stop him, and they don't necessarily come from outside his country. So he will have to watch his back all his life, and those of his children. His government knows this and will protect him as best it can.

Many people fear light, for it creates change. Change, to an old energy human, is the worst thing that can happen. Light exposes the dark ways of systems that were created to facilitate only the few, leaving the rest serving the few.

Light is what has changed the economy of the United States, spreading from there around the world. It is this pruning that we told you about over a year ago, even telling you that it would begin with insurance. It did. It is the first time in the history of a two-hundred-year-old economy that greed was taken to task. It has resulted in challenge for all of you but will eventually create a system that is stronger than it was before. Pruning is like that. Pruned trees look hacked up and dead. Then they come rushing back to life with a greater beauty than ever.

On the same subject, I am thinking about the Bush administration and particularly George W. Bush, who in the last year of his mandate received so much negative emotion from so many people. It is completely the opposite of what President Obama received. I cannot help but have compassion for this man, because it must have been very difficult for him.

Continue to have compassion for him. He is an example of an old energy leader who, to the end of his days, will feel he was right. But he was presiding during a shift of consciousness when almost everyone could see his old energy ways. He could not see this, and he never will. Here is an example for you to see, for many will not see the new energy and will fight the new ways until they die. This is the battle we spoke about years ago—one of old and new thought.

He became like the farrier doing an expert job of shoeing the horses, as the modern cars raced by. He didn't like the cars, didn't understand them, and was a horseman. Do you see? He believed in what he thought was the way, while many raced past his consciousness. He remains one of the best farriers, a true artist, but it does not serve him in a society that has stopped riding horses.

Two more leaders will fall soon because of this same scenario. Watch for this. They don't have real democracy in their lands, so their demise will be harder for them. But it will be for the same reasons. These are the potentials we see.

I think that we need to remember that certain persons are there to wake us up and that they too are part of the plan. In that sense, George W. Bush certainly did quite a job in putting the American people in a place of making a radical change but also gave every other country a glimpse at what is not acceptable in government anymore and at what is possible.

Could you elaborate on this aspect also?

You might say that he was like the abusive family member. These people come into a place where they have such energy that they make big change in people. Some hate them, some just get out of their way, but all are affected. Then some make life decisions because of them, and yes, some even find their spirituality because of them. Some even forgive them. {KRYON SMILE}

So indeed you can see that there is purpose for all of this, and one of them is for you to see what old energy is like during a shifting evolution of consciousness. The United States got to see all of this and made up its mind that it didn't want any more of it. Take a look, however, in that he was only perpetuating what an old governmental consciousness would have done. He was not that much different than the ones before him. But he took his seat during the shift! Do you now understand?

FOUR

AMERICANS NEED TO HEAR THIS

Now, let me speak to Americans about something they need to hear: I'm going to take you back about ten to fifteen years. During that time, America in particular decided to take to task the tobacco companies of the day. Citizens realized that the companies were out of integrity because they were trying to hook people—even children!—with a drug habit. So America decided to clean up its act, and it did.

Laws started to be passed that ensured that warnings were placed on cigarette packaging and that people were educated about the dangers of tobacco smoking, and these laws truly enabled the health of those who were not yet addicted, giving them the choice to examine whether smoking had integrity, and they did start to make different choices. Today everything is different, isn't it? What did the rest of the world say about what you did? They laughed! In Western Europe, when they saw what you were doing, they turned their backs and said, "These silly Americans. They're just so strange." They proclaimed, "That will never happen here." Well, go there today and you'll find the same laws you have!

Why am I telling you this? I am giving you this story because you are doing it again, allowing things to be cleaned up. First here and then later other economic systems on the planet. This is because you are the ones who can make these shifts first! You have a system that allows for *exposure without penalty*. You have a system that allows you to say whatever you choose, then examine the integrity of things that used to be what you would call sacred cows. The tobacco companies were one of them, and they fell in the process of your examination.

Integrity is starting to matter more and more in ordinary life. Dear ones, today you're in a financial crisis. But we see it differently. This country of yours is not in a crisis; it is in a pruning stage. What do you do to trees when you want them to grow better and survive? You cut off their branches, cut them down to the core. It's ugly! Then you look at them and you say, "I don't know if this thing's ever going to grow back." You do that, don't you? But the master gardener knows you've got to do that. He knows that when they come back, they're beautiful, aren't they? Bigger than before. Then you look at them and go, "Wow, that's amazing about nature!"

Well, let me tell you something that's also amazing. The principle of integrity in economics, when it is realized and used and manifested, is going to grow your financial system faster than any of your critics say it can be done. Are you going to sit there and fear it? Instead, perhaps you are going to realize that you have just *pruned the system*, and you're going to just sit tight for this winter. Let this winter be what it is and watch these things come back, for you have just done the impossible.

Again, these decisions were made by people in that good ol' boys' club from twenty years ago who said, "Banking is going to be this way. Insurance is going to be this way. That's the way we'll make the most money." You just called them on it, and things will never be the same. Ever.

What happens next is that it spreads. This integrity is going to spread into Europe eventually, and even into China. You're planting seeds in a place that was created for them—the United States. It's where you can do these things and nobody will slap you down for it. This was part of the potential of the very channeled documents of your country that were created two hundred years ago that give you that ability. Do you doubt they were channeled? Go read them etched into the walls of your past presidents' memorials. Cherish them. I've never spoken this way before. The system you created is a good one, for it allows for personal choice of human beings without penalty. If enough of you choose the right thing, the rest of the world takes a look and they change too.

It's tough, what you're doing, and there are some tough days ahead. If you go with me twenty years in the future, you're going to see a different kind of banking, a different kind of insurance, and it's going to be worldwide. This will be because of what you did here and now. What you choose to do and what your Congress chooses to do is, indeed, appropriate. Did you ever think of it that way? This is current information. That's what we want to tell you. Your situation isn't about anything failing. You know what just failed? Old energy just failed! The good ol' boys' club just failed. Greed just failed. So what are you going to do? You ought to blow up a balloon! You ought to have a party! I dare you to have a recession party! Why not? Look at the truth. Look at what's really happened. {KRYON SMILE}

FIVE

QUANTUM HEALING

In the last book, The Great Shift, *you talk about the coming of a fourth healing method (after energy healing, allopathic medicine, and alternative healing). At the time, you did not name it, but now I know that it is quantum healing. For the benefit of my readers, I would really like to better understand how we can put forward this quantum healing. Lee explained to me that it was "claiming the energy within our akashic record and going and getting the health that we had in another lifetime!" That sounds extraordinary to me, but if you start to talk about it, it must be something that is possible or about to be?*

From what I understand about this form of healing is that because all our lives are lived in the now, rather than sequentially in the past and future, we can access all the information from one of the lives that we are currently living.

If this is so, would it be like accessing our own hologram?

Yes, that is exactly what it is. If you are becoming interdimensional, then you are beginning to glean some of the quantum attributes that have always been yours. Accessing the akash is one. You have to understand that there is no such thing as a past life in a quantum state. They all exist in the now. That means that you are living them now. But only the "one on top" is experienced in the third dimension. But they are all there, ready to be used. You see them in time, as a linear stack. The truth is that they are all part of the soup called *you*.

At this time, are there some humans who can do this?

Very much so. Many in ancient belief systems are doing it! You didn't expect to hear that, did you? But the Buddhists and Hindus and Sikhs are some of the first to see the new energy and incorporate it into their lives. They already understand past life energy scenarios better than anyone else on the third-dimensional plane, for they have been working with them for centuries. Therefore, they have processes, meditative tools, and concepts that are ready to help everyone if you will look.

Do we choose which life we wish to access from?

No, this is something that happens automatically. You are the catalyst of intent that allows your Higher Self core soul energy to select what you need. Start calling this what it is: the innate within your own body. It can also diagnose any illness, point to the cure, and tell a complete story about what you need. Many are starting to use this more and more. It's new interdimensional self-help.

Doing such a thing, would that kind of healing elevate the vibration of all our lives, wherever we are?

Not really. You see, for a moment here you are slipping back into the third dimension in your thought, for you are seeing them as other lives. They *are* the hologram, so you are one with them all the time. There is no separation. Everything you have ever done with your own vibration also affects the entire hologram. So don't think of them as being elevated too. Think only of the whole being elevated.

I feel that you are giving us a map, but at this point we are still struggling to understand it... a bit like Michael Thomas from your book The Journey Home.

Will conventional medicine accept this? It sounds pretty far out for them.

Conventional medicine is always in transit. What was convention in the past is not today. Remember the first heart transplant? There was great objection from the church, wondering if the soul of the heart of one could exist in the other! Many objected to the procedure on those grounds. Now, that's laughable and seems like ignorance, but it wasn't that long ago.

Medicine will eventually accept anything that can be proven to work. When it does, over and over, then practitioners will have to take a look. They may never accept the idea of the akash as you do, but instead they may begin to acknowledge that the human body can mold itself and change its very attributes like they never thought it could. It will start the age of true body awareness, and psychologists will give it a name and create a process for it.

SIX

THE SEVEN

Recently, when I had a channeling, the Light Beings told me to do an exercise for seven days. Later on, another group also told me to do an exercise for seven days. From that, I started to ask myself different questions about the vibrational aspect of the number seven, going beyond numerology. This is what I discovered:

The number seven is one of the most important numbers in our history. It seems to be everywhere. We have seven chakras, and each chakra has a vibration of seven. Each cell in our brain has a vibratory level of seven, it seems from the research I've done, because in our embodiment we have the vibratory level of seven. Every life-form, if examined, has a vibratory level of seven. I have also often heard that a disease could be in our aura for seven years before it gets into the physical.

Seven is the level of creation of prime source. All life is based on seven. Seven is a multidimensional level. If we want to go through a portal—a star gate—we need to be at a vibratory level of seven. Every single dimension has a vibration of seven.

But what interests me most is that seven also seems to be a level of manifestation. If we focus on the vibration of seven, it makes manifestation seven times greater or faster. It seems that if we would focus for only seven minutes at a vibrational level of seven, we would be able to manifest anything.

Is this an accurate statement concerning the seven vibration?

Your concept of the seven as an energy is too simplistic and linear. Think of the hologram that must contain only numbers. So where does the seven fit in? The answer is that it is part of the system of numerology. No number by itself has singular energy. Numbers relate to each other very strongly, and the ones on each side, and also the ones used with them. For instance, the seven used with the four creates an eleven. Four is grounding and Gaia energy. Therefore, you can see that grounding (four) plus divinity (seven) create illumination (eleven).

So always think in number groups and what is above and below them. This is the true quantum numerology. The true core creative numbers of core universal energies, including all the quantum math of the Universe, is twelve. Now, twelve isn't even a number in numerological terms, so you might ask, how that can be? Instead, it points to the others in combination. Think of it as divinity (seven) plus change (five), or catalytic energy (three) next to new beginnings (one). You see? It's not of the third dimension! It's in a circle.

So begin to think of the seven as a *modifier of energies that work with other numbers* and energies to enhance whatever it is you are examining. There is much hiding here. For instance, you say there are seven chakras. Actually there are twelve, but you only see the seven that are in the third dimension. Do you wonder why there are twelve meridians of the body and only seven chakras? That's because there are more chakras than you think. There are twelve houses in the ancient system of astrology, twelve steps to the musical scale, and numerous other universal truths wrapped up in twelve. I only give you this so you will understand that seven is not core to anything. But it represents the divinity so many of you are discovering now, so it's an important modifier of energy around it. It, plus eleven, are the numbers of the age. Add them together and you get eighteen, the number of completion. See how this works? It always tells a bigger story than simply a single number.

Could it be a more powerful way to manifest? Is this the missing link?

Think differently about this whole manifestation scenario: The real number of manifestation is eight, not seven. But an eight can be divinity (seven) plus new beginnings (one). So you saw the seven as the biggest part, but it wasn't really. Take a look at your own life again. Wasn't it this way with you, Martine? You pushed the envelope of discovery for yourself some years ago and created new beginnings using your Divine Self. The result was manifestation! You used seven, not seeing the one, and created the energy of the eight. Do you remember that day? Think about it. Again, it's not in the third dimension, so it can never be about concentrating on one number or another. Think quantum.

Kryon, I read also that when we are in the fifth dimension, we will realize that we are multidimensional and we could experience immediate manifestation. We will stand in one spot and see all the possibilities: choice A, B, C, or D, etc., and choose the experience that we want to live. Is that a fair statement of what is coming?

It's time to get picky, but only if you choose to. {**KRYON SMILE**} If you are really going to think in a quantum way, then *there is no such thing as the fifth dimension*. Your reality is four dimensions: height, depth, width, and time. When you move to the next level of dimensionality, you eliminate linear things entirely, becoming quantum. So the next level is no longer something you can work with the way you are used to. It's not four going to five. In three-dimensional thinking, you move to the next level, but in quantum thinking there is no next level—for levels, layers, and steps do not exist. Numbering and counting don't exist either, because they are linear! Therefore, you can't count to five in the next level.

You see what you are up against? Your very thinking process is biased in 3-D. So instead of thinking about going to the fifth dimension (which doesn't exist), think this way: one, two, three, four... all? (quantum)! Just say, "You are becoming interdimensional" and don't try to assign numbers to next steps. It will assist you in getting out of your reality bias.

So how about when you start this process? Are there then more choices? The answer is not one you are going to like: no, because choices are linear (A, B, C). The true answer is that all possibilities and potentials become possible. You don't select them, but rather you absorb the combination of them that will help you to become an enhanced 3-D creature who is starting to become quantumly enabled. How? Your innate energy (Higher Self) will do it all for you, but only if you get out of the way and don't intellectualize it all. It's time to meld with it.

SEVEN

SYNCHRONICITY AND DIVINE INTERVENTION: IS THERE A DIFFERENCE?

About six or seven years ago, I was planning to participate in a spiritual event on a cruise ship. About two weeks before I left, I received a phone call from a lady in Europe asking me if I knew a book called Love Without End. *I told her no, but I would order it. Then, the day before I left, I received another phone call from a man asking me if I knew this book* Love Without End *by Glenda Green. I told him that I just received this book and planned on reading it during my trip. At this point, I knew something was building around this book.*

Then, during my cruise, I decided to go on a day trip in Jamaica. Because I don't like the tourist trap kind of outing, I decided to go by myself and explore the place. So there I was exploring quietly some little backstreet with these small shops really out of the way. I entered one and started looking around but felt that someone was looking at me pretty intensely and following me. At first I thought that this man was trying to pick me up, so I pretty much ignored him. After a while, he decided to approach me, and this is what happened next:

"Hi," he said.

"Hi," I responded.

Then he looked at me and said, "Do you know the book Love Without End*?"*

I looked at him in complete disbelief—how could this be? Not only that but I had the book in the bottom of my handbag! So I took it out and showed it to him. He did not seem surprised at all and said, "Great, I know the author. I can call her for you and let her know that you are interested."

"But I'm not finished reading it," I told him.

"Doesn't matter. I can still call her because I know that you will be interested." Then he said, "I can do that when we get back on the boat." And he did, and I never saw him again. It's like he appeared and disappeared.

And here's another story. At the very beginning of our business partnership, my brother and I didn't have a lot of money, like many companies that start out. At some point, we wanted to buy a contract for a book that we thought would be a good choice. But we just didn't have the money, so I decided to ask a friend to lend it to us. This was really touchy because this friend had had many bad experiences with lending money. So he told to me, "I will lend you the money on the condition that you reimburse it in one month, and I will charge you five hundred dollars interest." That was a lot of interest for a five-thousand-dollar loan! But we really wanted this book, so I accepted, pretty confident that we would be able to reimburse.

The month passed, and it was around the twenty-sixth of the month. I had part of the money but not all. At this point I realized that we would have difficulty reimbursing my friend. So on the twenty-ninth, we looked again into the bank account to see what I would be able to give him, but at the same time I was very disappointed that I couldn't keep my word. But then I couldn't believe what my brother told me: the money was there. We had a deposit to cover the loan and the interest! Even if I don't know where it came from, I understood that something was going on. Without hesitation, I drove as fast as I could to the bank, hoping that my old car would not break down before I got there. I just took the money out, telling myself that whatever the reason for it to be there, we would deal with it later. Of course, I was very happy to be able to reimburse my friend ... who decided not to charge us any interest.

Feeling a bit guilty, I returned to the bank later on, telling the bank teller that there was a mistake in my account. She told me that there was no mistake on their part and that we had two deposits for the same amount.

I looked at her, not believing that the money was really ours! Later on I learned that one of our distributors paid twice but never asked for his money back. He simply said that he would deduct the amount the next time. With that, we were able to publish one of our first books, Bringers of the Dawn. *That was very successful for us.*

My understanding of synchronicity is that it is a meaningful coincidence occurring within improbable coinciding events. It is the coinciding of realities—the seen and the unseen. It involves the nonlinear side of life.

My input on this is that in the first example the Universe was calling on me, and in the second I was calling on the Universe.

Is that accurate? Would you explain the difference between the synchronicity and divine intervention, if there is any? To me they seemed different.

Are these two situation examples of synchronicity but at a different level, or is one synchronicity and the other what I always thought: divine intervention?

What decides for synchronicity to happen, who decides? Does it start on the other side of the veil first? Or is it something more, something that starts in the three dimensional but involves the other dimension for it to take place?

These seem like two different energies, but they are actually the same one with different faces. Let's take a fun example: Many of you use the parking angel. You show up in a situation where there are no parking spaces and you are in a line of cars going around and around, hoping that someone will pull out right in front of you so you can have their space. That's the only way you are going to get to park.

The odds are about even for everyone, you are told, but you believe in synchronicity. So you call on the parking angel (your name for manifesting synchronicity) to help you. Sure enough, within a small amount of time, someone pulls out right in front of you and you get your spot. Now, who would believe you had manipulated chance? But you did! In fact, it happens so often to you that you know it works. It works so well that it is way out of the possibility of chance or random occurrence. In some cases, it's actually scary, because it happens so fast, and you never tell your unbelieving friends what you are doing. After all, who would believe it?

I am saying that this is an example of you *plugging into the holographic system of potentials*. God (Spirit) cannot tell the future of what humans are going to do, yet so often prophesy is correct. This is because Spirit can see the most profound potentials lining up. It's a puzzle of immense proportions, and you can't even consider what that might look like—the potential decisions of every human on the planet, interfacing with each other all the time. It's a glimpse of free choice at work.

So what you are asking for is to be placed at that perfect spot to intercept what Spirit sees as the most possible potential manifestation of someone who is leaving ... and it works!

In your first example, synchronicity was being created by the book, the man, and the author. Spirit knew the potentials of them being together and allowed the person to be in the place that would most benefit the situation.

So did Spirit do that? The answer is no. The author, at some level, had been asking for these things, a meditative allowance for her to be plugged into the system for the most benevolent outcome—and she got it. Often the human then wonders what happened and thinks it's a miracle of confluence, but it's simply an answer to a prayer or an intent to move forward in your life. *Synchronicity is an answer*. It doesn't happen by itself. Remember that so that when it happens, you will look at it that way. What do you do when you often see 11:11 on the clock ? Do you wonder? Or do you nod and thank Spirit for allowing a wonderful wink and hug that you are, indeed, never alone? It's never coincidence.

The banking experience is not divine intervention. *It was you, creating a synchronistic moment of overpayment!* To Spirit, this is simple energy. To you, it was divine intervention. Was it divine intervention that you had the book to publish? Was it divine intervention that you got the loan? The answer is no. It was your Higher Self starting to learn how manifestation works ... something that you now understand pretty well, don't you? [KRYON SMILE] Did you ever wonder how it could continue for so long and so well? Was that also divine intervention, or was it you learning the system?

Dear ones, this is an example of becoming interdimensional in thought without understanding how it works. But you know the principles, feel the energy, and make the correct decisions. This is you learning the system of potentials and working with it.

Who told you to write this series of books? Divine intervention or an intuition? You know the answer, and in the process tens of thousands of humans have been able to read these words and find solace in them. See what you have done? Now, tell me: who did this?

Let this be a profound lesson in self-examination: The human is the source for change on this planet. It is the human who makes the decisions to move left or right, not God. It is the human who can learn to create a parking angel who can park them over and over in places of abundance, peace, love, and appropriateness. This is what we teach.

Humans collectively made the synchronistic choice to put a Lemurian Indigo into the White House. Think about it and what it means for your age.

EIGHT

HEALING OF A CELLULAR MEMORY

I think that, at this time, more and more people are experiencing or will experience memories of past lives. Not all are coming back up, but some are. I think that those that need to be healed are the ones that come back up.

For the benefit of the readers, I would like to share an experience of a cellular memory that came back up in 2004. I presumed that it was healed because it came up and I was made conscious of it. Here is the story:

I was at a seminar in Italy in 2004, and one of the teachers said, "This morning we are going to go into a past life." Upon hearing this, I said to myself, "Going into a past life!" Frankly, I had trouble believing I would go into a past life simply because someone said so. So I decided that I would simply relax and let the others do it.

As I was simply relaxing, I suddenly saw a white screen coming down in front of me. Then I saw words slowly being written: "1870... Billings, Montana." Then I clearly saw pictures appearing on the screen. An Indian woman—I was this woman of about twenty-seven years old, and I was talking and laughing with my husband. We seemed very much in love.

At one point my husband said that he had to leave and go hunting, so I went with him to the end of the village and watched him as he left. I stayed there, waving at him until I could not see him anymore. At the end of the day, I went back and waited for him to return... but he didn't. The next day I went back and waited, but he didn't return. I went to the end of the village every day for weeks. I waited and waited for his return … but he never came back! I was completely devastated. I never remarried. I just hoped that he would come back one day. The others in my tribe told me that he had probably gone to another village and remarried. I didn't believe them, but I felt great sadness.

Fast forward…

Then I was now around seventy years old and about to die. I felt relieved that I was dying because I could finally know what happened to my husband. I told the person who was with me at that moment just before I died, "Now I will know what happened to him."

So on this screen I saw myself dying… then leaving my body and floating in the air. And then I saw him. He was hunting, aiming at something, and he had to step back. He stepped back, back and back… and then he fell! There was a cliff, and he didn't see it or he didn't realize that he was about to fall. He just died there alone at the bottom of the cliff. Nobody ever found him. I waited for him for more than forty years to come back, thinking all those years that he had abandoned me! I was there in the astral plane just looking at this scene… feeling so much sorrow and sadness for him… for me, in seeing what happened. I stand there for a long time looking at him at the bottom of the cliff, as if I still could not believe what I was seeing. Then I see myself going toward a light…

When I left this memory, I was in front of everybody and crying my eyes out! It was like it just happened, and I felt the grief so profoundly inside that it simply exploded.

Before I left for Italy, one evening I was with someone whom I loved very much. When we separated, I remember looking at him leave and the scene seemed so familiar… I looked at him for a while wondering if I would see him again. From my understanding, something that evening triggered or activated this memory for it to come back.

Kryon, I know that there are as many scenarios as there are cellular memories, but, for the benefit of my readers, could you explain what happened for this memory to come back, the reason behind it, and how our past lives, present, and future are all connected?

Did it come back because I was reliving a similar situation, the same scenario of seeing someone leave? Or did it come back because it needed to be healed because I never properly grieved the loss of this man that I loved dearly?

Was the person that evening the same as my husband in my past life, and is that the reason watching him leave had such an impact?

So now, my dear one, we really get to the issues, don't we?

The most profound issues of a human being are around love. Love is the most powerful energy of the Universe. It doesn't hold a candle to hate or jealousy or anger. Love creates the passion of lifetimes, writes the greatest music, and paints the greatest pictures of the centuries.

Your lifetimes are selected and lived by you, and you do it in a circle around things you wish to learn, or wish to revisit, or wish to reexperience. Sometimes you select challenge so it will help others. Sometimes you come in to die so that parents will find their spirituality... all in love. Sometimes you lose someone you love in one lifetime and decide to carry that challenge into life after life, *but allowing also synchronicity to hook you up again if you discover how to manifest an answer.*

When you discover a person who lives alone, doesn't need love, doesn't want to have it, or doesn't seem to find it, you are looking at someone who won't go near that energy for a lifetime because he or she lost it and simply doesn't want to go through the experience again—better to live alone. That's a powerful akash, wouldn't you say? You *all* have something like that.

Is this a vision of a real life of your own? The answer is yes. The quantum reality of it is happening now, and it has affected your relationships ever since you left that one. It has kept you from creating the kind of synchronicity you feel you wish you had. Did you ever wonder why partnering is sometimes difficult for you? Now you know: *you are afraid he will disappear, and the grief is soaking in your akash.* You would not ask these questions, dear one, unless you were allowing personal answers.

I want the readership to understand that the akash has this kind of powerful energy. In addition, you are always looking for this same energy in someone, and there is a secret: in this lifetime you already have found it. Keep reading, dear one.

"Well, Kryon," some may say, "when you drop the duality and void karma, doesn't it all go away?" No. What goes away is the energy to fall into the karmic groove and continue lessons of the past. But the influence that your past lives have on you remains. That isn't karma. It's residual energy from past life experiences. Sometimes it represents a continuation of a life of art, as in the case of obvious child prodigies. Sometimes it creates beautiful people and sometimes evil ones. Sometimes it creates fear of love, and other times it creates a wonderful balance and a lifelong partnership.

So here you are, Martine, with an akashic energy that is with you at a level you didn't realize. Another answer for you: Your friend in this life was not the one in that life. He just brought the feelings up again for you. I'll tell you a secret; place it in the book if you wish. The man you lost over the cliff is your current brother. This was Spirit's way of saying you will never lose his love for you. It is a permanent relationship that helps you to have the male love energy in a way that is stable. It is your reward in this life for waiting so long in the old life. Now you know how Spirit works in these cases. Meanwhile, the energy of what happened is so prevalent that you continue to come in as a female until it is dispersed. It will disperse simply by human expression—lifetimes—but you can also get a fast track on it by starting to become more quantum, which you have been doing.

For all of you reading this, clearing these things is not linear. Voiding karma doesn't make the akashic record go away. It simply disables the energy of unfinished business with others, lessens your propensity to fall into the groove of what your sister did, your mom did, or anybody else did.

In your case, you are now out of that groove of karma, creating your own path. But the energy of the akash is always with you. Don't think in a linear way with these things, for they don't fall into convenient boxes for you to work with.

In the book *The Journey Home*, we taught that Michael Thomas got rid of all his karma in the house of gifts and tools (the second house in the book). This was all a metaphor for what we are now teaching. He learned to void his karma, and he then reached into the akash and found a life where he was no longer afraid of tight enclosures or heights. He actually customized who he was through this process. This is the process of quantum healing, and it's not just a healing of disease. It's a healing of certain akashic attributes, the ones that keep you from going forward. So for you, Martine, there was no fear of abundance or success. You created wonderful synchronicities for that and accepted them as you went. This is you, out of the karmic groove, creating what you needed.

Now, the invitation is open for you to void out this vision and all the grief around it. Start by rewriting the scenario. If all humans have a hologram, then your brave Indian husband never really left you—he was there all your life, watching you cry.

Quantum human beings will learn to look at things this way, and after an appropriate time of grief they will carry their lost loved ones in their pockets for the rest of their lives, loving them, talking to them, and knowing that they will be with them soon enough. He is with you now, and he never stopped loving you, even in death. So you see? You were never alone. Take this to your heart, and it will slowly void the whole experience so that you may move forward in this area if you wish. It's time for a fresh approach to love.

NINE

IT'S IN THE DNA

Let's talk more about the akash for a moment. First, let's say that the akash is an energy that represents everything that is. The akashic record, therefore, is a record of all that has been and more. The concept of the akash represents all that is and the potentials of everything that can be. In the three dimensions, the akashic record is an archive of things accomplished. However, it is also a record of potential things unrealized.

There are two kinds of akashic record: one is global, and one is personal. The global one is contained in the Cave of Creation. It is a physical place on this planet, filled with crystalline energy. You might say that every single human being who is reading this has a crystal in that cave. That's not exactly interdimensionally accurate, but it's the best we can give you in the three dimensions. This makes it simple for you to visualize. Each of you has a physical object in this place that is sacred, crystalline, and stays on this planet after you are gone.

The hard part about this explanation is that this crystal is timeless. That is to say, it carries with it the core energy of your Higher Self when you are here on the planet. When you are not here, the energy of this object is placed upon the Crystalline Grid, which is global. All that you ever were on this planet is imbued, permeated, to the grid. Therefore, you might say that your Higher Self still resides with Earth. At some level, you would be right. This also explains how a human can talk to the dead, for in a timeless state everyone who ever lived is still here, within the crystalline.

An Overview of Coming and Going— The First Kind of Akashic Record

When you come into the planet, you activate this unique personal crystalline structure, and your Higher Self is then responsible—the caretaker—for this crystal while you are here. The Higher Self of each human is always on my side of the veil, but it has tendrils, you might say, that allow parts and pieces of it to interface with you and the planet. These are the parts that you get in contact with when you meditate. Once you arrive on Earth, the energy of the Higher Self is connected to Earth for as long as Earth exists.

The life that you live right now becomes etched upon this crystalline structure. The decisions you make, spiritual and otherwise, all the things you experience, what you go through as a human being, all are imbued to this crystal. The properties of crystalline structures are well known in your science—minerals that have an atomic structure with long-term atomic order. This creates a unique attribute discovered early, which is that of memory. In our case, it is way beyond anything your science will ever have ... a crystalline structure that contains sacred life lessons, knowledge, memory, and remembrance. What you don't realize or understand in the three dimensions is that the crystalline also has the potential of the future imbedded within it. Difficult to explain, isn't it? Let's keep it simple for now.

You live your life on Earth, and when it is complete you experience what you call death, which we call transition. You then come back to the Cave of Creation for a moment. At that point, everything you experienced and learned gets sealed into this crystalline object, and then your Earthly essence and the personal sacred portion of your Higher Self leave the planet.

You might say that this crystalline record is like the rings of an interdimensional tree. It places upon itself a lifetime at a time, everything you learned and all that your DNA has collected. This is far more profound than you expect, for the changes that have occurred in your awareness, if any, remain on this planet in the form of vibratory shift. It remains here for always, because it is placed onto the Crystalline Grid of the very Earth itself. Therefore, you might say that the very Earth resounds with your vibration—past and present.

Nothing is wasted; nothing is lost, dear human being. What you do here stays here. All the things you did, all the decisions, all the epiphanies, the love, the joy, the drama, and the sorrow... they're not just for you, they're for the Earth. The vibration of the Earth itself, therefore, is made up of the trillions of lifetimes of energy created by humanity for approximately fifty thousand years.

It's not a time capsule, for it's active all the time. A time capsule is passive. Interdimensional things are always in the now. Therefore, there is no time stamp on any of this. It just is, and is seen by, the planet as always current. That means that whatever you experienced is still being experienced and is fresh.

After a period of Earth time, you may revisit the Earth. Most of you do, for a lifetime on the planet is like a day in the life of a grander scheme. The grander scheme is an overview of hundreds of your lifetimes, and Spirit sees you not as a human in this life but as a timeless, sacred entity that is part of the family of God, working for Earth—one who has been here over and over in different incarnations or expressions of karmic energy. This is very difficult for you to understand and accept, for you think life begins at birth and ends at death. That is no more true than a perception of life beginning at dawn and ending at dusk. It continues and continues, and each life is like a day in a grander life. You continue to awaken and sleep, over and over.

You have called this process reincarnation, when an expression of your Higher Self again comes into the Earth. It's the same Higher Self for everyone, by the way. Think about that for a moment... many lives, many faces, both genders... same Higher Self. It comes in as it has before and places the new energy as a beginning addition into your crystal. You are then born on this planet, and you continue the journey seemingly as someone else. Then you live that life. When you're finished, what you experienced and learned becomes another *ring on the crystal*. Over time, this sacred crystalline structure is imbued with hundreds of rings of lifetimes. One Higher Self, many lifetimes, many names and faces ... all *you*. That is the essence of the Cave of Creation and the process of the Crystalline Grid. It's how it works. Whatever you do stays here on this planet and contributes to the energy of all humanity that will follow.

That is the overview of the akashic record in the Cave of Creation. The difficult part to explain is how it also contains the future, for the potentials of all the lives you may live are also on the Crystalline Grid. It helps to posture who you'll be the next time around. I cannot explain this to you, and I'm not going to try, except to say that there is purpose in all these things. Many have called it karma, a continuation of unfinished business, much like waking up tomorrow to the errands of the day that you didn't get to yet. The errands wait for you... they are the future. But in the case of an interdimensional energy they have always been there, and they will affect what you do when you wake up.

The Second Kind of Akashic Record

There is also a mini-akashic record that occurs in your DNA itself upon birth. It is shaped in the womb and given at birth. This is the akashic record of who you are and who you have been on Earth. It also contains the potentials of what you might do, carried within the layers of the DNA within you. This may sound like the same attributes of the crystalline record in the Cave of Creation, but it is not. The record in the cave is for all humanity. It is connected to the Crystalline Grid of the Earth. The purpose of the one in your DNA is personal discovery, awareness, karma, and life lessons.

It is esoteric. It is even odd to you, isn't it? Some may even call it unbelievable that in your DNA is the record of who you ever were. We're going to talk about how it affects you, what it means. We give you all these things in a small amount of time, condensed into this message today.

Some of you are asking, "Well, Kryon, right away there is a puzzle. I understand what you're saying. You're about to teach the fact that we come in with many energies from the past. But what about the first-timer on Earth? They have a crystal that has no rings, you might say. It has no energy of past expression, no past experience on Earth. So what about that? What happens then?" This is a very logical question. There is a well-known energy of a newcomer that is unique to the planet. Most of you reading this have experienced it. Also, there are many newcomers! Know this: Kryon is very aware of geometric progression. That is to say that the human beings on this planet grow exponentially in number. As the population grows, that means, dear human beings, that there are many, many first-timers, for whatever the percentage of those who are old souls, there's an even higher percentage of those who have never been here. We know that. It's part of the plan and the energy of Earth. So this message does not apply to those who have never been here. At other times, we have discussed the attributes of the first-timer. You are beyond that.

Mining the Akash

You might ask, "But, Kryon, how can we change our akash?" I'll give you the first step: *You've got to believe that it is possible.* Don't believe it because I said it's there. You've got to believe it so strongly that it's as real, biologically, as your arm. When you look at your arm, you say, "I have an arm, and it is there, and I can see it." There's no question, and your brain knows it too. The matter around you knows it, and to prove it you can pick things up with it. There's no question about it. It's your arm.

Now, how do you feel when you say, "I have an akashic record in my DNA. I have a record inside me of all that I ever was, which I can access." Tell me what parts of your body object to that statement. I'll answer—*all of the linear ones!* Logic will yell at you, "You can't do it. You cannot change who you are." And it will be wrong about that.

You can all do this. It is part of being in this new energy, and I want to tell you that many who are in this room have already changed it. It can be done slowly and in small increments. It can be done quietly with nobody noticing, and it can be so obvious that your best friends no longer recognize you. The energy for this comes from the storehouse that is you. It's in your DNA, every single piece, trillions of cells that all are synchronized to your will.

There are three levels of difficulty in changing the akash: easy, medium, and difficult. I will tell you what happens in each one. Do you understand the premise? Do you understand, human being, that you're not asking God for anything? What you're doing is changing yourself to the degree that you can go in and get what you have already learned, what you already worked for. The key? You have to understand and believe that the *one* Higher Self was with you each time. That means that your central consciousness was involved in all of them. You are *not* a different entity this time around. You are simply another expression of the same Higher Self. Therefore, you were there for all of these things we are speaking of. You have to believe it. The Higher Self has been waiting for you to bring in the belief.

Easy: Fears, phobias, and blocks. They're easy to clear. Yet these are the ones everyone wants to change and has trouble with. How would you like to not be afraid of whatever scares you? We'll talk simply here. Are you afraid of stepping forward, afraid of change, afraid of what's happening around you?

Some of you have phobias. That is to say, these are holdovers—hangovers from past life experiences. Are you afraid of heights, insects, water, this and that? You may say, "Well, yes, but it doesn't really affect my life, because I've learned to live with it." Yes, it does! It includes darkness in a study of light. It doesn't belong there. You don't need it. It interrupts your belief, your efficiency, your progress, and you are constantly aware of it. It's not *you* this time around, because it reflects another lifetime ... from somewhere else. You don't need it anymore. It's like trying to be quick to change clothes but having to carry around a bunch of old baggage that you claim you never need to open and use. Does this make sense?

So begin. Start to work with what you now believe, in the same way you *believe* in your arm. Soon you find that the phobias and fears start to retreat and change. As they do, you start to reclaim that part of the akashic record that you used to be. It feels just like you. It really *is* you. It doesn't feel like anybody else, for you are just claiming what you already own. The fears start to go away too. You can feel it, and you can continue to challenge them and work on them so that your cellular structure feels it too.

Afraid of heights? Occasionally go to a high place to check yourself. You'll see how the fear starts to become less. You are no longer paralyzed to look over the edge. These things start to go away to the point you will wonder why they were ever there! These are small challenges. The blockages from you moving from one energy to another are real, but they will subside as you claim the power of what belongs to you—lack of fear. It's growth, and it takes practice. But you will absolutely see the progress.

Humans don't like to change. Many of you have these blocks of awareness. What is it that triggers your anger? It's a block of peace, isn't it? Can you eventually be patient while a fool speaks to you about his foolishness? Can you be understanding instead of angry about his process? Yes. These are the simple things. You can pass these tests, change your life, and then start to work on the more complex issues. The beauty of it, dear human being, is that if all of you did the simple things, you'd have a group of peaceful warriors—warriors of the Light. You all would be unencumbered by fear, phobias, and blocks. You would all send light with purity, and there would be no judgment from Spirit if you do nothing else. But if you wish to do the work, the tests get harder.

Medium: How would you like to get rid of your allergies and change your immune system? It's a little harder. You might ask, "Well, how do you do such a thing? Do you just think it away? I either have allergies or I don't. My cells are allergic." Oh, really? I'll tell you, dear ones, some of you reading this have dropped their allergies because they realized they were holdovers of something they didn't need anymore. They went into the akashic record, and they got the pristine DNA from the one lifetime when they were never allergic to anything! That blueprint is still there! It represents an immune system that was hardy and whole and never had disease. In that lifetime, they were strong and never allergic to anything. How would you like to not have sickness? How would you like to have strength and energy beyond your years? This is harder, but it is so. Whatever you think you are can be rewritten at the cellular level.

How would you like to have peace over everything in your life, no matter what? I didn't say the problems would go away. I just asked how you would like to be peaceful about them. How would you like to get rid of the drama and the worry? Drama issues are interesting: when the Lightworker does not *work karmic energy*, drama disappears! When you drop your karma, there is no reason to continue the drama about something you don't need anymore.

You might say, "Kryon, I dropped my karma years ago when I decided to change my path. This sounds like it's still there." It's not that simple. Giving intent to drop your karma is like clearing the path before you. But now you have to get up and walk that path. The karmic attributes shout at you: "Pick me up! I'm yours!" But then you remember as you walk the path that your intent has created a situation in which you never have to pick those attributes up. But they will always be around, talking to you.

This is difficult. Let me tell you, old soul, the Lightworker reading this, you have been priests, you've been nuns, you've been shamans. You've gone through these things or you wouldn't be reading this esoteric information. In these medium akashic attributes, you might say, you can develop a personality that is so peaceful that everybody wants to be with you. That is the answer, is it not? This is the peace that the masters had. This is only the medium part, so I've just given you the starting point. Now, I'll tell you the hard part.

Difficult: This is the unbelievable part. This is for the one who really wants to dig into the akash and change the future. In each of you is all that you ever were, eons of experience. In addition, if you're going to mine the akash—that is to say, if you're going to go in and get these things—you will be voiding the things that you don't like about this life. That is the result. It's not that you're going into the DNA and getting something different to paste upon you. Actually, it's an exchange—one for another. That's the way it works, for the DNA claims everything you are. What you are doing is exchanging attributes, putting into the record what doesn't suit your energy and claiming the things that do. You own them all.

There is something else: Each of you has what we call a spiritual jar. That jar is filled with everything you have ever learned as a human being on this Earth about God, guides, angels, interactions, sacred communication. And the jar is *yours*. It does not have to be refilled every lifetime. It lays there ready for you to unscrew the lid and pour out everything you ever knew. It is part of the system of the spiritual akash. It is the spiritual gilding of all that is, allowing a seeming novice on this planet to become a master overnight.

This novice paid his dues and lived through it. Perhaps he even died for his belief.

Many of you are afraid of certain things because you died as a result of them. Some of you don't want to touch the esoteric because it carries a fear of enlightenment and death. Your fear is such that you don't want to open the jar. Many will reject this entire premise, not believing. Well, not really. You believe, but you just don't want to touch it again. I know who's reading this. So the first attribute in the hard category is opening the spiritual jar and placing upon you all that was ever learned by you. Are you afraid of this? Some of you were important in the history of spiritual things. That's the truth.

Not only do you carry spiritual knowledge, you carry in the jar the persona of who you used to be. This is difficult to explain to you. Overnight, seemingly, one who is not interested at all in metaphysical things may become a prominent teacher. Out pours the jar, and all he has to do is learn and listen to use the information in a linear fashion. Nonteachers become teachers. Those who had no knowledge at all now have great knowledge. Those who were clueless have great wisdom.

The spiritual jar—that's the hard one. It's there; all of you have it.

You can assume a personality that is completely and totally different than the one you were born with. Are you ready for that? Are you too attached to the fears, phobias, and blocks? Would you like to have a more peaceful personality? That is a fear in itself, is it not? You might feel you are losing yourself, only to find yourself! It's available in this difficult category. These are the things that can be given with clarity through connection with the Higher Self. Growth in these things requires a greater communicative ability from the human being to the Higher Self. Each step gets you more connected.

I can hear you questioning: "Wait a minute, Kryon. You said we were connecting to our DNA, not the Higher Self." Yes, I did. Where do you think the Higher Self is? It's in the interdimensional DNA. We even gave you the information of which DNA layer contains it and the Hebrew name for it. We even told you its number was six: the sixth energy of DNA. That core information, that Higher Self, lurks in trillions of pieces of the DNA all working together to create who you are. Your Higher Self is not some angel in the sky. It's inside you, imbedded in your cellular structure. There's so much here to know.

You may say, "Kryon, I'm confused. Where is God in all this?" Right where you would never look—God is the concept of a loving family of spiritual help that is somewhere beyond the veil. God is love, yet you can't really find that fullness outside of you. It is a constant search, and humanity has been looking for God since creation. Now I again reveal to you that the system of God is inside you and that the very essence of your divinity lies in the interdimensional DNA that is within your own body. Be still and know that you are God. Let the search stop and celebrate victory in finding the truth in the most unlikely place: inside.

We're almost done. How would you like to have talents that you do not have now? "Kryon, how can that be? I'm either talented or I'm not. I either play the piano or I don't." How 3-D of you! There you go, deciding that it's finished. You feel like you are some kind of cake, and when you come out of the oven you're finished! You don't understand that you are just the beginning recipe, and that recipe shouts to be altered. In your akash—that is to say, in your DNA—is the remembrance of talent that you don't think you have but that you did have. This is again called mining the akash. We've spoken of it before. It takes years. It's doable. It can happen, and it can be awakened. What are you afraid of? Why not begin now?

You say, "Well, I cannot speak in front of people. I'm not good at that." What about the orator in the third century? Are you going to throw him away? After all, he was you! Would you like to go in and get those attributes? The orator speaks with authority, and people listen. That's a talent. Many of you have this within you yet didn't when you were born. Therefore, you can't imagine such a thing. You can't live that many lives without having this talent. I'll say it again: There's such a variety of what you have in your own history that you can pull upon it, dear human being. It's yours to develop. Too strange? Ask my partner someday about it. He did it.

The hardest one: how would you like to change your DNA to such a degree that the disease that surges through it now won't even remember it was ever there? Go in and get the clean DNA that you had *before* the disease ever arrived! The DNA remembers what it was like. It was participating, remember? Begin to change your own DNA in an interdimensional fashion so that the disease will retreat, go away, and never come back. "Sounds like a miracle, Kryon!" Indeed, it is... the miracle of shift into mastery.

Miracles are only things that are outside of your normal belief. Change your belief, and miracles become ordinary. Sometimes when these *miraculous* things occur, humans lift their hands to God and say, "Thank you, God!" There is no understanding that they have activated their own DNA to such a power that they received what only the masters could give in the past. They simply exchanged what was theirs to exchange, in a nonlinear way. They healed their own life. What was only thought of as available from the masters is now available to all. This is the enablement of the human race. Less than one-half of 1 percent will ever do it. But you are part of that group, and you know it.

We would not tell you these things unless they were so, unless they were accurate. We have only opened the door to a teaching that should be expanded.

There is a system here. It's a system in which the energy of family stays with family and you don't even know it. There are those here in mourning for those they've lost, yet they've not *lost* them at all. In linearity, you don't understand the love of God or the system that is here for your benefit, for your enhancement. These who you have lost will hold your hand the rest of your life. Don't you see? It has to be that way. It's your solace. It's where your peace comes from. It's designed to help you through life. It's family!

There is much hiding here, and the system provides for you to begin to access the akash. Push on the door. Take the hand of your Higher Self and never look back. That's the invitation, old soul. That's the invitation.

Blessed are the humans who read this.

TEN

THE MIRACLE OF DIVINE FORGIVENESS

Kryon, this is the story of one of my best friends. With her permission, I would like to share it with my readers. I would like you to comment on it, explaining the process that took place.

She is one of the rare people I know who seems to understand the word forgiveness. *Here is her story:*

Last year, her husband was waiting at a red light. A drunk man fell on his car, provoking some kind of altercation between them. Thinking that everything was over, her husband left the scene.

About a week later, he read in the local newspaper that the police were looking for a man involved in an accident! Recognizing the event, out of honesty, he decided to go to the police to simply explain what happened. But that is where his whole life changed—and the lives of his family! The police arrested him because the drunk man fell down afterward and was now in a coma! So at that point, they did not know if it was an accident or an act of aggression.

Nobody knew exactly what happened because the man could not speak. Throughout the ordeal, my friend would repeat to me, "He's just a poor man, and I forgive him. Everything is just an illusion." Event though she was very scared for her husband because, if this man died, her husband could face a very serious charge and its consequences, she never budged in her faith.

This lasted for weeks. Finally, the worst scenario seemed to be happening. The man in the coma was disconnected from the machines that kept him alive because the doctors said that he would not come back from his coma. Everyone in her family was devastated to learn this.

My friend kept telling me, "Whatever happens, it is all an illusion, and I forgive him, and I forgive myself." And then the miracle happened. Even though he was in a coma for weeks and was disconnected from life support, instead of dying he woke up. Not only did he wake up, he was fine! He did not even remember what happened that night of the accident. Because of that, all the charges against my friend's husband were dropped. He was cleared, and the man just continued his same way of life like nothing had ever happened.

Kryon, to me this is one example of what could happen when one understands the real nature of divine forgiveness but also that all is illusion, and we can change the illusion if we get out of the drama.

In this example, we had the worst scenario—a man dying and all the consequences—but also the best scenario of all and its rewards. It is almost like it did not happen. Not only that, but it was not even my friend's life that was in difficulty, it was her husband's. I think that the whole thing is very powerful.

Could you explain what took place and how such a great outcome came about? My friend is convinced that if this event had happened ten years earlier, the outcome would have been different because she did not understand how things worked then as she does today.

Yes. Consider these things a dance of energy. What she did in her perspective was *allow for the energy of the awakening of the man*. Can one human change the life of another? Not directly, but through posturing of their own reality, they create a bed of potential for another to work in.

For instance, if you built a path and people walked upon it, did you make them do that? The answer is no, you just built a path. They made the decision to walk on it. But the potential of them doing it was good, wasn't it? See how this works?

Her forgiveness and acknowledgment of the illusion before her created a path whereby the man came out of the coma. This is profound, for now you might understand how one human working in light on this planet can change the lives of so many around her. She doesn't make anyone *do* anything, but rather she creates an energy that is so attractive that many are interested and helped by it.

Get used to this, for it is the center of how you create your own reality. As you create what you need, it involves others, but also know you can't control them! So now you know: *Your light creates a path, which others can walk... a potential that often leads to a win-win situation with many people as you create your own life.*

ELEVEN

AN AMAZING REAL-TIME CHANGE IN ENERGY

The October 13–14, 2008, Event

Dear ones, in October 2008, there was what you would call a *potential prediction*. I can speak of this now because October 2008 is gone.

The science of prediction is well established on this planet. For more than a decade now, those in a university of learning, particularly those part of the Human Consciousness Project at Princeton University, have discovered how to make certain kinds of devices that react to human consciousness. Because human consciousness is interdimensional, these devices react before events happen! You might say they are able to pick up the randomness of potential. This is not a secret, and even my partner has reported these things in his lectures. It's an interesting study about the energy of humanity, and futurists love these machines, because the machines start to react *before* potential things happen. The scientists saw it happen before things like the 2004 tsunami in Asia and even the death of Princess Di—both worldwide compassion events.

Recently, these indicators were starting to signal something happening. They read that something in the world consciousness was sensed before it would happen. It was centering around the middle of October 2008. What they were beginning to pick up was a shift and that it would take place on October 13 and 14 worldwide. It was major. The Earth moved on an interdimensional level. Did you know that? You say, "No, I didn't," and that's what I want to tell you about.

How do I describe this? Humans tend to linearize interdimensional potentials in their own belief systems to make it viable to the 3-D mind. Thousands of human beings were convinced there was going to be a landing of a giant flying saucer on the thirteenth or fourteenth of October. Out of that flying saucer would come wise entities from beyond your planet. This ship would be the biggest imaginable, and it would be reported by the entire Earth. This group strongly believed in this potential, as it was a collectively perceived vision. They published it and counted upon it.

This was the best story they had to linearize an Earth shift. It was expected. They linearized it completely to make it 3-D and make sense. They had a ship landing from afar and wise entities helping all of you. I tell you right now, there is nothing wrong with this. It's the best thing they had to make sense of what they saw. Did a ship land that the entire Earth reported? No. *But were they right?* Yes. It seems to be a puzzle. It didn't happen as perceived. With so many involved with this prediction, what went wrong? Were the scientific instruments right? Yes. But you didn't see anything, did you? Let me continue.

I told you before not to fear changes that were coming. This was one of those changes, and Kryon saw a challenge coming. For I see the potentials of what is there, and I was not the only one to channel it. Seemingly from many sources and many places, you heard the story, "Beware of October." If you do the simplest kind of numerology on the thirteenth and the fourteenth, the thirteenth becomes a four.

In numerological terms, a four is Earth energy. If you do the numerology on the fourteen, it becomes a five, or "change." Therefore, what was to happen was Gaia—Earth—change. You were expecting an earthquake. A big one. A global one.

Like the tsunami, which was actually so large it changed the rotation of the planet, this event would do something similar and create global shift. Now here's what you should know: *there is an old energy paradigm that connects Gaia to human consciousness*. Every single shift on this planet that has a consciousness vibration alteration requires some kind of physical event on the planet. In this case, it was going to be an earthquake—movement of the planet's crust. That's how connected human consciousness is to Gaia. Now be careful, my partner, because I want you to get this one correct. Let's go slowly.

Listen carefully: on these dates of October 13–14, 2008, this planet moved in an interdimensional way without the expected challenge. All the sources, including the ones on my side of the veil, expected something larger than what took place. We didn't expect the human consciousness had raised to a place where nothing physical would happen. *It's the first time this has ever happened. A major shift of this planet took place without the challenge of disaster and without the challenge of death.* Understand that this old energy connection had to do with compassion. And the only way to generate the kind of compassion needed for a major shift was for the kind of thing you all were used to... but it didn't happen that way.

All the predictions were there. What about that saucer landing? Well, in an interdimensional way, this planet has been imbued with more wisdom from the ancients than ever before. Without any challenge, without any Earth motion, the needed compassion was also delivered. Well, did a landing occur? In a way, it did. For now this planet is vibrating higher than before. It is a consciousness shift that normally would have taken physical planetary involvement, but you slept right through it, didn't you?

Blessed is the human being who slept through it, because there is a new paradigm happening: change without challenge. This is the goal, but it can only be accomplished if human consciousness is at a higher level than it was. Now I can tell you that it won't be that way every time, but it was this time. Things are moving quickly, and even the best futurists will be taken aback by the lack of visionary consistency—for that's what happens to a timeless object that is always in vibratory transition.

Again, the incredible human being shocked us all, just as it took place in 1987 (the Harmonic Convergence). The shift is working. Less than one-half of 1 percent of you need to make an awakening to create peace on Earth. Many cry, "Oh, Kryon, how soon?" It's up to you. But things will happen faster than you think, and all you have to do is look inside to enhance the process. Free the light that you carry. It's about self-discovery.

TWELVE

THE GREAT COMPASSION EXPERIMENT FOR 2010

Kryon, I think that we should all be humanitarians at this point in time. In that sense, I've been having the urge to create a grand movement—a compassion movement.

I want to create a network of ten thousand people that will put out an intention to participate together in changing the world through compassion. I really do think that we will be brought together though compassion.

I want to reunite ten thousand people to change the lives of one million people. It would be about the rising of consciousness through action. Many projects would be involved, especially returning power to women and dignity to children. One thing is for sure, our sisters all over the world are in trouble, and it is unacceptable that this situation continues. If we intervene on behalf of women, children will automatically benefit.

Like many others now, I just feel this strong calling to do something: to be of service to each other, changing things, changing lives together. Not just talking about change, doing it.

I feel strongly that within the energies of 2009, such a project could come to life and maybe have some kind of influence on the world. I'm doing it even if I am alone, but when you have a lot of people on the same track, change can come about faster. I certainly have the audacity to hope.

But even more than this, I realize that this experiment could change not only the lives of the people who receive our intention but will change us, the ones participating, even more. I really want to try this and see what a group of people can accomplish together. One experiment with one intention.

Kryon, I would like for you to comment about the power of intention when ten thousand people come together to change things. What would be the power of such a group?

Am I dreaming the big dream? Is the new energy ready to support such a project?

Is it fair to say that such an experiment would in fact be multiplied by ten thousand because it would be supported by all our higher selves?

Yes. This is the way such things work. There is actually an accelerator that occurs when many human souls decide on such a thing. There is the energy of magnification due to the quantomization of the intent.

Know that this project has come about through your own process and not a message from God. All decisions that affect the world come from human thought just like this one. The energy is ready for something like this right now, but there will be a tendency to make it linear—organizing and thinking about something all at once. That seems like a very good idea. It's been done and was nice, but now you sit in a whole other energy: *one that is nonlinear*.

It's time for a quantum group that dedicates a space of consciousness for this so it becomes them. Then it isn't a scheduled thing. It's a consciousness thing. The other side works with you through the magic of the system of potentials (again). It aligns thought with thought and amplifies the intent of a group—even one whose members don't know each other, don't look at the clock for a meeting, but rather agree to be compassionate every moment they can think of it.

Build it. They will come.

Are we really transitioning from working alone to working together? Would this be an example of a project that could teach all of us how to work together without being together physically?

Any input about this would be greatly appreciated because it seems complicated and simple. I'm scared and I'm trilled at the same time, but I know that I have to do it.

That's the exact idea, dear one.

THIRTEEN

THE POTENTIAL AND PROBABILITIES OF 2010

Current Events

WEATHER

We have some simple advice about the weather. Understand that it's not going to get better. If you sit and wish for it, that will not make it better. We have explained it before, so we will say it again. You're in a water cycle that is profoundly set to create a *mini ice age*. It may seem odd to you that it gets hot before it has to get cold, but if you look into your geology records you will find the exact same thing has happened before. You didn't have the same record keeping back then in the 1400s as you do today, but it happened then, and you survived it then. So we say to you, the winds will return, and our advice is to prepare for this by creating a situation to acclimate to the new. Learn to anticipate it; build differently. Feel free not to build where danger is or learn to build in safer places.

But the admonishment is this: Don't be shocked when it returns. It will return. Don't be surprised when the levees break again in the South, because they will. You'd be much better off to move the dirt around in that town and build on higher ground. In this berm system, you build houses on what look like large striprows of raised dirt, where only the streets are below the water level. The houses are all built on the dirt strips, emulating the way crops are watered. That is smart. We'll see if it happens. "What are you saying, Kryon?"

I am saying that human beings can adapt as they have in the past and the way you can now. If you start thinking smarter, you can adapt for the weather changes. Take charge of how you affect it, not how it affects you. Turn weather catastrophes into weather events.

Also, do not fear what is happening. Do not project what you see today into some kind of drama that you expect tomorrow. The warming is a precursor to cold, just as in the past... just as in the past. You can sit around and worry about it, or you can prepare for it.

THE SCIENCE OF SEEING INTERDIMENSIONALITY

In August 2008, a grand experiment took place. The largest machine on Earth started to study the smallest things that exist, things that are invisible. We speak now of the large atomic accelerator in Switzerland. There are many who have said, "This is dangerous." It is not. No more energy will be created there than is present in the barrage of cosmic energy that hits the Earth every moment of every second. All they are doing is creating that same energy in a controlled way so that they may study it. They cannot study it when it's random.

They use protons and antiprotons, and they speed them up to 90 percent of the speed of light. Then they crash them into each other in the largest physical experiment that's ever been. Let me tell you what the potentials are, and remember, you heard it here first. {KRYON SMILE} What they're looking for is interdimensional energy. They are looking for what they suspect must be there, and they will find it—because they're looking at universal creative energy. Let me tell you the profundity of what they're about to discover within this next decade: they will rewrite the scenario of how the Universe started. The Big Bang never was (as we have discussed with you many times). The very idea of the Big Bang is a three-dimensional explanation of an interdimensional attribute. Universes are created all the time through interdimensional shift—when one dimension literally collides with another. It's a grand quantum event. This is when you get all the attributes that you describe as the Big Bang.

A review: In 3-D, you had many scientists looking at what they felt was proof of the Big Bang theory. They had found the residue of what they thought was proof (cosmological constant). Names like Hubble and others were at the forefront of this. However, this is now about to be challenged by the observation of the smallest particles known.

First, even the Big Bang theory had to be interdimensional at its beginning, for there is acknowledgment that everything traveled faster than light and everything happened all at once. Back in the days of this theory, it was simply understood that somehow there was a break in 3-D for a moment in order to create what you see. Today that would have been seen as an attribute of a quantum event, and that's what this laboratory will discover, for they are about to see the residue of an interdimensional collision. It's everywhere. It's the new cosmological constant. Once you begin to see the dimensions that are invisible or at least see the attributes that they trace in the explosions that are artificially created, it will be obvious. All of this is to say to you in this cryptic way that this particular experiment is safe, long term, and your science will finally be able to see interdimensionality at its best.

When nothing happens and the Earth is not swallowed up in a black hole created in Switzerland, will you remember this message? Will you look at those who said otherwise and hold them responsible for the drama they created? We shall see.

When there are things on this planet that you need to be warned about, then watch for a consensus of warning from all of us. Remember HAARP? [Kryon, Book Six, 1997] We warned you, and you responded. This experiment was seen as dangerous by most of Europe, and steps were taken to regulate what the facility could and could not do. When many are watching, it is very difficult to accomplish secret things. Remember this:

The energy of thought on this planet is shifting.

Is the *energy of thought* a current event? Yes, it is, and it is shifting greatly, just like we said it would. Humans are thinking in a different fashion. Many of them are starting to have understandings and epiphanies, even about science. New thinking is afoot about how things work. We told you they would eventually do this.

Those who will never be esoteric are giving you esoteric information, and they're calling it science. Discoveries are being made that will lead to interdimensional thought. Science is being rewritten as to what is real and what is not. All of this is in line with what we told you about the potentials of this planet.

Now, how does that reflect in the current events? You're on the cusp of something, and I will tell you what it is. Dear humanity, you really can have peace on Earth, but there will be gyrations that you will go through in the process of learning what you want and what you don't want. It started in 2008, then continues in 2009 but also in 2010. There are some potential events for you to watch for.

The year 2009 is an eleven year. Eleven, numerologically, has many kinds of meanings. What it means to you in old numerology doesn't matter. Eleven is the number of this age. We told you that when we showed up. In 1989, I gave you, in the first transmission in the first book, the meanings of eleven. Now, here you are, coming up to an eleven year yet again (2009). Only this one is the last eleven you're going to get before 2012. That ought to be significant to you. It's the only eleven with this energy. Here's what I'm going to tell you: *Watch for the young people of this planet to make differences in the next few years—differences you don't expect from youth.*

One of the biggest is the potential overthrow of dictators. This is the potential we spoke of when we told you the chest-pounding dictators of this Earth were on their way out and would be replaced by benevolent leadership. It is the beginning of a shift of consciousness of what political leadership should be and what ordinary human beings are going to expect from their leadership.

In old energy, government was simply tolerated in many lands. Without it, there would be chaos, so whichever kind of government was created in your land was acceptable. That is an old energy concept, for it led to those who would be in control without integrity. That's going to shift—in your own land as well—for human beings are going to start to expect leadership with integrity. That is new. Watch for it.

In 2009, there's a potential for a major shift in a country that I'm not going to mention, but it's going to be caused by the young people of that country. Those who you would never feel could even care are going to rise up and make a difference. Watch for it and when you see it, don't look at the news and say, "This is bad." Don't look at the news and say, "Look at those who died." Don't look at the news and see the drama. I want to tell you there are those who have come to this planet just so they could be part of that very thing and return home, then come back and do something even greater! I want to tell you the overview of how this is far grander than you think.

Congratulate those who have decided to pass on for this reason, for they made a shift that is heroic. That is what we see. The whole planet is involved in this kind of celebration. It really will change the future. Can you celebrate appropriateness?

A GLIMPSE AT THE NEXT TWO GENERATIONS

Let me tell you something: the first thing you're going to see in these next two generations is change regarding things you thought would never change. Many of those who are reading this will say that what I'm going to tell you is impossible, for what we are speaking of is a change in *basic human nature*. How do you treat each other? What do you think about one another? What do you think is correct and right? What's the first reaction to challenge? Drama, jealousy? There will be a tempering of the things that are inappropriate in life. These items represent duality, and that duality is changing.

There will come a day within two generations when things won't be what they are today. Here are some examples of what we are talking about.

Leadership

Eventually this will be reflected in leadership within governments. Leaders will be elected because of their compassion for those around them and for their good ideas for those around them, not just because they're popular or charismatic. Can you imagine a change like this?

Can you imagine a change in common sense? You say, "Well, wait a minute, Kryon. Common sense is common sense." No, it is not. Common sense is dynamic: it is simply your idea of what naturally works within a current consciousness. What happens when a consciousness changes? So do the attributes of common sense. I tell you that if you could attend some meetings in fifty years of what they think common sense is, you'd be alarmed. It literally defies what you think is going to happen. Look at what has happened in the last thirty years to America—what you have been able to openly discuss, talk about, and change. Look at what you've just done with your country, against all odds of what was formerly considered cultural human nature. Now, just do it again! Amplify it. I will tell you this, that the whole idea of human nature and common sense is going to change and so is the goal, the very goal of your being.

This is what is before you. It has to do with cleaning up the integrity of all things within your society. What have you seen in the last year? How many leaders have been brought down because of things discovered? Have you noticed? Is there something infectious going on with integrity issues? {KRYON SMILE} The answer is yes. It's about time, and you know it. Let me tell you, there're three more leaders who are shaking in their shoes as we speak. You'll see. It's time to call them on these things, is it not? And you're doing it.

Terrorism

"Well, Kryon, you haven't addressed the big one. Terrorism." I suppose you think Kryon doesn't know it's here? I'll give you some information you didn't expect to hear: *You're not going to beat terrorism with terrorism, ever.* You're not going to beat an old energy force with force. It just isn't going to work. Try it. You'll fail every time. As you put out one fire, another will develop somewhere else. It's perpetual failure.

Here is how you're going to beat terrorism: with new consciousness from new humanity. There'll come a time on this planet, not too far from now, when the very consciousness of the idea of terrorism will not be palatable to the human being, for he will know better. The more it doesn't work, the less there will be, for it won't create the desired result anymore... and that's common sense not to keep doing it. Terrorism won't even create fear! Instead, it will create disgust even among those who formerly felt it was the only way. Do you see what I'm saying?

Africa

In two generations, Africa will arrive as the biggest competitor on Earth with a huge economy of its own, one that will rival even that of China. No matter what China does, no matter how many people are there, this new economy is going to successfully compete—for China is slow to move and must plow through its own historic consciousness to get there.

There is an entire continent ready to be healed. It is rife with war and civil strife at the moment and has been since you were born. It is sick, but it's not going to stay sick forever. Millions and millions of individuals are involved, and they don't know it yet, for like almost everything else it is against all odds.

What happens when you heal a continent? You'll see, for it's about to be healed. When it is, those there are going to discover that they can build an economy as good as yours, because you've set the standard! They're going to start by looking at you. We're speaking of Africa. We're speaking of the potential of a group of states, eventually, who will emerge called the African Union or something similar. It will be a bigger conglomerate even than the United States, made and patterned in the same way, with an economy created in the same way. Millions will be involved almost instantly.

What you solve here in your recession is what Africans will observe as the energy they begin with. This is different than other emerging economies. Many of those begin and grow and walk through all the mistakes you made during your growth. But the Africans will not go through the gyrations of the first two hundred years as you did. They will see America and take from you what you teach them. This healed continent is going to want what you have. Africans are going to want to have their own affluence and their own banking that is free from major greed. They're going to want to have all of the things that make a society grand and great, and they won't have any problem funding it. Many stand by to create a new society where there are borrowers for businesses and homes. Once you take millions and millions of people who are no longer in survival mode, they want homes, schools, factories, and land. Watch for it. It's inevitable. It's going to start happening while you're still here. Look at what has happened in China despite a noncapitalistic government; now amplify this idea for Africa.

A New Tolerance

There'll also be a renaissance in a very old Eastern religion and a respect like never before. There will come a time when the idea of killing in the name of God will be seen as barbaric. Instead, the idea of Eastern religion will be to evangelize those around them with systems that work and ideas that create harmony and attract converts.

Tolerance will begin to take hold mainly because young people will become the leaders, and those young people will have a conceptual plan that is very different from the old energy. They will absolutely know that violence does not create peace. Other fundamentalists of many other religions who have previously made themselves known due to their violent ways will also start to find that violence creates no new converts—only harmony will do that. Based on what you have seen, you think this is crazy, don't you? It's going to start changing. Give it time. But it isn't going to happen without Lightworkers, dear ones.

We will use an expression in your culture: "What happens under the hood, nobody sees." That's you. For the more light you put on this planet with what you know—touching the Higher Self, staying around longer, picking up the akash—puts light on the planet for the rest to see that was formerly in the dark. That's how it works. That is always how it has worked, and now you're starting to define it. So you will understand why you're here.

This is the beginning of a crossover of energies, and you're right in front of it, dear ones, and you are here for that reason, every single one of you. Listen: There are those who are reading, who have gone through horror in this last year. I want to tell you, I know who you are. There is an expression, "Iron sharpens iron." Like the blacksmith who pounds the piece of iron while it's red hot so that it will become a tool when it cools, you are being shaped. Then that tool goes on to make other tools, and those make other tools. We know what you've been through, and we congratulate you for coming out on the other side of this with the light brighter than when you started.

Will 2010 bring us closer to ending duality? In the meantime, how can we work on this aspect of ourselves? Through compassion?

As we see it at this time, every year brings you closer. However, know this: it's a very slow process. Look at how long it took for the United States to change. Some say eight years ago had an entirely different consciousness of leadership. It took that long, because these things are slow. So you can't expect things to change overnight. Compassion is the key. Look at the new leadership (Obama). His compassionate nature and what you see in his speeches are overwhelmingly attractive to his audience. Compassion is the key, and few leaders have really had it. Many speak of it but don't actually have it. He does.

Compassion is a result of becoming more quantum, looking inside, and asking the question, "God, are you really there?" The answer will be yes, and it will always come with a love wash and a realization from the ones asking that they have received an answer! What follows over time is an increase in compassion.

It's part of an evolving consciousness. Take a look at the masters of the past. All of them featured compassion.

I think that we all agree that human consciousness is going somewhere it never has before. But human consciousness is just part of what is going on. Every plant, animal, rock, or tree is being fitted for a higher light, a new program of return to prime source.

Does this mean that every sentient being will receive a new program within its own biological family and receive a new hologram, one with a different memory bank?

There is a Master Syllabus at hand, a plan for humanity that you set for yourselves from 1987 to 2025. That's thirty-eight years and is an eleven in numerological terms. You might say that it's a complete reprogramming of human nature and the energy of Gaia. It coordinates with the Crystalline Grid, and it's something that I will reveal soon.

So the answer is a gentle yes, but one that will happen slowly, just like the shift of consciousness that you saw elect the new American president. Nobody can point to a time when that happened; it just seemed to come about slowly.

The different memory bank is not a new one, but one that begins to remember the positive things in the akash and not be driven by the negative ones—an entirely new direction for humanity.

From what I can see, 2009 is a year of partnering but also of continuing to let go. We seem to be in a perpetual state of spring cleaning, but I feel that 2010 will bring a better understanding of significance of this transition.

What is the greatest potential that 2010 holds for us? In 2008, you talked about a major event that could change a lot of things. Is this on schedule to happen? What about the Middle East?

The major event already happened, and it's a setup for 2010. You asked about it, remember? The new president. It happened in 2008; the numerological equivalent of that year is a one. One means new beginnings, so you are right on schedule with what I told you.

The year 2010 is seen as a year of catalytic energy. Yes, there will be an event, and it will create compassion. Don't worry about it or try to analyze this, for it's only a potential. What if it were positive?

You don't know what the potentials are. Whatever happens will help to boost the next step in the Middle East.

Now, who told you to ask that, Martine? Sometimes the potentials sit there so obviously that it is known in advance of the answers!

FOURTEEN

IRAN

*Kryon, in early 2007, for the second book of this series (*Going Beyond the Veil: The Illusions and Confusion—2008*), I asked you a question about Iran. This question was to understand how information coming from two reliable sources could be so different concerning that country.*

For the benefit of the readership who didn't have the chance to read about it, here is the question and part of the answer.

Kryon, in Lifting the Veil *you talk about two countries. You said that we will be surprised to see wisdom coming from these two parts of the world: China and Iran. But in another book, one I consider a reliable source, it is mentioned that the next nuclear bomb will come from Iran, of course affecting humanity at a grand scale. To say the least, it is confusing for us.*

There is no difference in the prophecies of doom and gloom regarding Iran than those regarding the Soviet Union. In fact, the mechanics are identical. Back then, the Russian people were not the enemy, but their dictatorial leadership was. When the leadership dissolved, you may have noticed that there was no end battle. You might have noticed that it happened from within and that the Russian people were the ones who brought it to an end. They were the wise ones who took it upon themselves to change history, using the light from all the others on Earth who joined them in this endeavor of peace. No battle, no death, no bomb… and the West was left in amazement.

The people of Iran are very wise. Many of them are young—younger than the average age of your civilization. They don't have the number of older ones you do, so they think differently. And rather than being all radical and ready to vaporize themselves in some kind of final battle for their God, many are instead silently wondering how to bring their leadership into check while still maintaining their faith. Many wish to create a situation that might bring them abundance and a more peaceful life within their region.

Make no mistake. They are not allied with the West, nor are they about to be. That is not their desire. They love their own lineage and their own Prophet. But they wish to change the idea that they are all disposable martyrs, led by their older ones who seem to be ready to take them to the brink of destruction.

They have the kind of resources in that small land to bring wealth to almost every citizen there. Their wisdom, therefore, is that of the peacemaker and the industrialist. Their great Prophet taught them unity, and yet their governors are seeking division at the highest level, against the karmic lineage of the planet (Jews). *{Editor's Note: Kryon always said in his writings that the Jews are the karmic lineage of the planet. As goes the Jews goes the planet.}* These citizens of Iran are witnessing the foolishness of their leadership, and there is much fear among them that they will lose their lives and their country… and they may be right if they do nothing. Here is free choice again.

It is May 2009, and I am listening to one of my favorite shows, 60 Minutes. *One of the segments is about Iran and how it is changing.*

The reporter said that a big part of its population is under twenty years old and that they want change—they want freedom and don't want to be known as terrorists, etc. They were speaking from another city because they could not find the freedom they wanted to express themselves in Tehran. When I heard that, I immediately remembered what you said about Iran. It was happening. We were seeing the awakening of Iran, but I never thought I would see this so soon! They expressed themselves with such passion and wisdom. They had hope.

A month later, we had the election, and then we saw bigger changes. Even if the door seemed to be shut again, for a moment it was wide open and we could see the entire country through this open door, letting the world see what was happening and letting us know that Iran will never be the same.

I was following and reading anything I could on the situation, about what I felt was a grand transition taking place. I read in Time *magazine about one young woman saying, "We want our votes to be counted because we want reforms, we want kindness, we want friendship with the world..."*

Another woman had a peace sign that read "Only Mousavi." She felt that what she was doing for her country was much more important than going home and making supper for her children. She said, "What I am doing is much more important for their future." At one point, some people told her that she might be beaten for speaking so openly, and she said, "Let them beat me. My country is going to waste—what am I worth in comparison?" Right at that moment, it seemed that a Basiji charged at her and was prepared to strike her... and then another miracle took place. A group of men got out of their cars, tackled the man, and started beating him! They were defending her!

Again, the fact that we are seeing courageous people willing to risk their lives to make changes in a country like Iran tells me that this country has crossed a threshold.

Kryon, would you please comment about what I call the awakening of Iran and the courage of its people? It seems so miraculous, and I almost feel that Iranians will show the way to other countries, even though things have calmed down there and they are still stuck with the same old energy leader, Ahmadinejad. It is just the beginning. I am sure that it will not take fifty years.

How can we help them consciously to attain their goals?

Dear one, what you have now seen is indeed the soft revolution* that we spoke about. We should pause and examine what really happened, because history is filled with situations like this—short-lived, only a moment of unrest until the authorities take control.

This is far more than that, and it will not stop. The seeds have now been planted, and all the desires of these young people—having been openly and honestly presented to their leadership—have now gone underground. The leaders had a chance to change their country, to keep their power, but they failed. An old consciousness, however, keeps them from seeing that they have failed. In their eyes, they have won the battle. But like melting snow, the springtime of a better year begins to erode the biggest of snowbanks, and the leadership is doomed.

The potentials are now set, and Iran will begin to shift. The majority of the population is now poised and waiting for the moment to take control, even if it means replacing their aging spiritual leadership by force, which they will. Time takes its course, but under the seemingly controlled society there is an awakening new energy of hope and purpose that will eventually change Iran completely.

The new energy has given this kind of thing far more power than at any time in human history. This is the difference, and you can watch for it. Two major dictatorships are also potentially set to fall over for similar reasons, with the result being not a replacement dictator, as has happened historically, but instead a system that gives power to a representative government. Remember, free choice is a spiritual concept and not a political one.

Again regarding Iran, rather than a rogue state who wishes to fight a Western system of nonbelievers, these young people would much rather have their own system that is complementary to the rest of the world, complementary to their faith—and one that opens itself up to free commerce and the hope of freedom of choice for the majority of those who live there. There are many Islamic nations that do this, and it does not disturb their faith or change the teachings of the Prophet. For again, He was about unity. For it is a compassionate God that he spoke of ... one who loves all of you.

Iran has a most amazing history and has contributed greatly to the culture of that part of the world. It is beginning to reestablish itself as a viable player that will actually help to stabilize that portion of the Middle East instead of pull it apart. This creates the possibility of a powerful Iranian renaissance. Can you see the incredible irony in all this? What was defined as an "Axis of Evil" instead becomes a player in the potential of stability for a very profound area of the planet. Can you see how this might eventually affect Israel? Ancient enemies are beginning to realize the core family within all of the strife. They are not likely to be friends for generations, if at all, but they are starting to realize that to eliminate the other one only perpetuates suffering and hardship for all their lives. The focus is beginning to shift to tolerance.

Patience is the key, as it always is in this new energy, and restraint and the sending of light instead of force is the task of the day.

*A soft revolution is Kryon's definition of anything short of civil war, or a dispute that splits nations, such as the conflicts in Korea and Czechoslovakia.

FIFTEEN

WOMEN AND CHANGE IN THE MIDDLE EAST

Empowerment—It Is Time to Speak

I know in my heart that women are, by nature, problem solvers. They always seek to resolve conflicts instead of creating them. I think that the best hope for sustainable peace in the world is women. We have seen it in many African countries, like Liberia, Burundi, Sierra Leone, and many more. We rarely hear about it, but it is a fact well documented when we look more closely. These women go beyond political parties, religious differences, and ethnic backgrounds to speak in one voice and to resolve problems, try to put an end to wars in their countries for their children.

I think the same thing is happening in the Middle East. Women are gathering together and creating change. The media won't let us see it, but it is there. They prefer to let us see the conflict rather than the efforts for its resolution... especially coming from the women. I think that Afghanis are the forerunners to a new generation of women leaders. So much of the war pattern in the Middle East is based on lack of the sacred feminine energies.

Would it be fair to say that, because of that, women who are incarnating at this time in the Middle East are the ones carrying a special key to the sacred feminine, to put into form the divine feminine so that peace can eventually take place? I think that within their DNA, a special key for compassion is present—much more there than places that do not have the conflicts or war. Is there a plan of compassion in the Middle East through women?

Dear one, it is the meld of the God and Goddess energies that will be the key. Women carry the gentle task of compassion, so indeed this is the energy that will begin to be needed all over the Earth, especially in those areas where the Goddess energy is not even realized. So the women are needed to carry an even bigger compassion than before, helping those in their specific cultures to shift.

Peace on Earth is only possible when there are many compassionate humans—not when one gender is submissive and one is in control. This old system served its place and time but can no longer survive. The systems on this planet that have this as their cornerstone will find themselves crumbling under the pressure of the new energy.

But know that these special female ones, who you indicated might be incarnating at this time, have actually been incarnating for the past twenty years for this purpose. This is what you are seeing that makes you believe something is different. The shift that is happening right now in this part of the world has a major push from these quiet ones, who have come in for this very purpose. You are seeing it everywhere. But what is actually happening with the akash at this moment is different than you think. Instead of more souls incarnating as women in the Middle East, the opposite is true. Women are coming back as men, and men are coming back as women. This will create a system in which there is more compassion balance, for there is nothing that women can do alone to change this planet. Men must take on the sharing of the mantle of compassion—something that mothers have known since the beginning of time. The men must change an old system, and you have felt this, Martine: that Goddess energy—the compassionate female energy—is the key. So you might say that reincarnating souls are more aware of this than ever before and switching roles to help accomplish balance.

Remember, DNA carries all past life experiences within, so attributes of immediate past life energies are very strong in incarnating humans. In addition, the new energy on the planet is creating a system where historic protocol is beginning to lose over new thought. This means that the meld of God and Goddess energy will be more prevalent than ever, creating things like soft revolutions. {**KRYON SMILE**}

So there would be a joke for women on Earth that would go like this: *Women are paying the ultimate sacrifice ... coming back as men!* The truth is that all souls play gender parts that switch through the ages, but right now, your intuition is serving you well, for something is indeed happening with the akash regarding the Middle East, and it is being celebrated as it is happening.

After all, the purpose of the whole system is to see how much consciousness can change human civilization, and the track record in the last twenty years is showing that it can.

SIXTEEN

CONCLUSION

Kryon, I often think about this phrase: "If you want enlightenment, lighten up." Would lightening up help us with this transition?

Yes. Lighthouses, strike your lights (light them up)! This is the lightening up we need. When any human beings begin to examine themselves, it creates energy. This energy is seen by Gaia and the Crystalline Grid, and the intent of it collectively goes into the planet. This real-time effort is new since 2002 and creates an accelerated attribute of how humans create light on the planet.

Call it a cooperative energy if you wish, but you have never had this before in this way. Does it get you out of duality? Yes, if you consider duality as the kind of dark/light attribute of the old energy. Light brings you out of ignorance. It starts to make people see the difference between religious mythology and spiritual self-awareness. This is the real battle you fight: to bring new energy to an old energy humanity.

The year 2009 is the year in which this book is being written. The year 2009 is an eleven. That is a master number that means illumination. It's created with two ones back-to-back. The one is new beginning. Do you see the significance? It's not an accident that we are now talking about creating illumination through self-awareness. This will continue to be the theme of my teaching for the next few years:

Change yourself... change the planet.

And so it is.

PART TWO

THE SIRIAN HIGH COUNCIL

Introduction by Patricia Cori

Gaia, our beautiful Earth Mother, has entered a phase of violent upheaval. The *gentle* way, apparently, wasn't enough to wake us up to her needs, as we have been so focused on our very specific desires, at the global level, in our race toward materialism and might—a race that seems to have led us nowhere, if not back to ourselves and the search for meaning in life. It seems we need to take ourselves to the ultimate brink of disaster before we move, as a global force, toward resolution.

In this hour of planetary rebellion, she has begun to demonstrate violently to her entire community of the living how very clearly we are now careening toward something immense, unprecedented, and yes—at times overwhelming. The planet, under our misguided tutelage, is in desperate shape, struggling to overcome the reckless abuse of her most "intelligent" species—man. This we simply can no longer deny.

We see so much breaking down: lifestyles, our morality, all that we have created as the structures of our societies, nature herself. Those of us who have been around for a few decades often glorify the past, a time when life seemed easier and less "dangerous." Yet, deep down inside, we know that that is an illusion. To cling to what was and to wish to return to what some describe as "the good old days" is to be blind to the enormous possibilities that lie before us, often overlooking the beauty of *right now.*

There, it appears to me, lies the essence of duality: *on one side of the polarized collective mind, the waves of emotion resonate to fear of the unknown; on the other, they vibrate with the higher frequencies of wonder (for what we are capable of manifesting) and celebration.*

Some fantasize about the past and those so-called "good times" we have known, desperately clutching a fantasy of what can only be remembered as "better than this." Others project into the future, forsaking their responsibility for the world right now, hoping that some magical wand will be waved and we will be free of our own karmic imprints.

But let the truth be known: throughout our written history, we have never known a Utopian existence on planet Earth. There have been moments of greatness, the human will rising to the challenges of life, just as there have been those of despair, where humankind has seen the dark shadow looming over our existence. Moments of absolute tranquility and peace, at all corners of the globe, have never been recorded and most likely have never been lived.

The very nature of the 3-D experience, the physical Universe, is one of polar opposition (and attraction), electromagnetic interaction, and the entire spectrum of possibilities in which the free will of every soul is perpetually faced with the choice between the darkness and the light. That is what we came in to experience; that is what we came in to learn. And that, fellow seekers, is the purpose of our lives—no matter how our personal situations and the global reality tend to veil that ultimate purpose to us.

Choosing the darkness simply holds us to the wheel of reincarnation for as many more lifetimes as it will take to release ourselves and proceed upon the spiral of light. Choosing the light, on the other side of the pole, hastens our progression back to Source. In the end, it is so simple that it escapes us, leaving us swinging back and forth, like pendulums, in the world of duality.

It is up to us, free souls, to determine how we will resolve this polar opposition at the Earthly level as well. As a community, we are faced with the opportunity to shift the entire planet to the light, a process Gaia is preparing for now. However, let us not be passive: she needs our help to make that shift as gently and as lovingly as is possible, in the field of probable realities through which we are now finding ground.

At this moment of our explosive reality, we do realize that change is urgently needed, just as our spiritual growth is the way of the future and that death, which we so fear, is only one of the ways through which we experience our immortality.

As we enter 2010, we are head-to-head with the extreme challenges of our time: the massive destruction of our ecosystems, the extinction of hundreds of thousands of animal species, global financial "collapse," war on almost every level.

How we perceive these changes determines not only how we will live, as families and individuals, but how we will experience what lies before us, racing through the years that precede the fated date of December 2012 and the experience that follows it. It determines what Gaia, herself, will create as a reflection of our awakening to our own creations—however dark, however light we manifest them on Earth.

We are experiencing a peak in the intensity of the breakdown of the old, from which the new emerges. Pushed from our comfort zones, we cannot help but question the meaning of life—the mission—and to then take those much-needed steps toward healing the planet, to which we are ultimately dedicated and connected.

At this hour, we are being directed, managed, and manipulated into absolute survival mentality—a mentality of fear, isolation, and obsession with *lack.* Gloom and doom seem to sweep the entire human race, and yet, at the other side of the shadowy world of illusion, huge numbers of our collective are waking up not only to the mechanics of such control mechanisms but to the amazing potential of immense change as that which we face today.

That is not to say that one is blind to suffering. It is all too obvious that many people are struggling just to survive and that this struggle, which has always represented the world most of us do not see up close and uncomfortable, has now extended its reach to our space—to our neighborhoods—where we, the fortunate, have enjoyed (and abused) so much of the world's abundant food, wealth, and natural resources.

We are facing our creations, and most of us don't like what we see. The question is: are we honest enough to assume our responsibilities for what is so out of balance in our realm—or do we blame everyone and everything else for all that is falling down before our eyes?

My incredible experience as channel to the Sirian High Council has taught me, more than anything else, how important it is for each of us to accept our part in the unfolding of our reality and to strive to make it better... to make it perfect... every day of our time here on this great Earth.

To release ourselves from the roller coaster of experience, whereby we are plagued by fear and hopelessness, we are given the opportunity (at the global level) to understand it—once and for all.

Do we fall to our knees in obedience, throwing aside everything that we have demanded from our governments: our right to freedom of mind, movement, and speech? Do we allow ourselves to be fooled into believing that we are powerless before change? Or do we stand tall, uniting forces, reaching out to the other—to help and to share? Do we speak our truth, as perhaps we never have before, knowing that is the way to our true liberation? Do we serve others, as light seekers, helping the lost to find their way back to that light?

These are questions of our time. This is the path to our resolution of duality. And by the Gods, this is the moment of our greatest opportunity—let us live it empowered: One Heart, One Mind, One Soul.

—Patricia Cori,
Scribe to the Speakers of the Sirian High Council

From the Sirian High Council

The time of the Great Shift is upon you. It is stirring within your elevated perspectives upon the fields of Gaian experience, just as it is stimulating your awareness that a new paradigm for humanity is unfolding right now, before your eyes, as the old breaks down to make way for the birthing of the new. It is a process that lies within you, the microcosm, just as you move through it—the macrocosmic vortex of universal evolution.

You are spinning rapidly now, experiencing the palpable transmutation of the space-time continuum: for some this elicits a sense of exhilaration; for others, one of trepidation. You know, at the essential core of your conscious and subconscious awareness, that how you understand the immensity of this process can only be determined by where you have focused your thoughts, which then determines where you are focusing your energies. This focus creates manifestation for every soul as an individual unit, which inevitably affects and determines the condition of the oversoul of planet Earth—and beyond, where all sense of separation disappears in the glorious Flame of Divine Oneness.

We know how much you desire a concise Book of Transcendence, spelling out the language of evolution, impatient as all can be to take the giant leaps of spiritual evolution, as a species and as individuals on the path of enlightenment. Perhaps that search for definitive answers (to an infinitely unanswerable question) is born of the fear and anxiety of what you perceive lies "ahead" of you—as well as the need to define and give meaning to the enormous changes taking place in your Earthly landscapes.

Like a map to the rainbow bridge, which leads to that elusive pot of gold, such a complete book of instructions for the interdimensional ascension of souls has simply never been written. The immensity of that process is beyond the word—beyond even universal cosmometry. Its breadth reaches so far beyond the physical Universe that one can only glean shimmers of its light through the sages and teachers of your world and others, who bring illumination to the endless realms of consciousness throughout the multiverse. It permeates the ethos through the vibratory frequencies of Light Beings, ascended masters, angelic spirits and beings, like us, who have already transitioned, helping you to open your minds to the possibility of what lies beyond your conscious awareness, but which has always been yours—lying deep within you. The rest, beyond those potentials, you acquire as you mount the stairway to the galactic center.

It has never been written, nor shall it ever be, because we create it as we go, climbing the great spiral of light, where all hearts are nourished in the luminescence of the One Heart. However difficult it can be at times, along that infinite journey, to recognize that all creation exists as a stage upon which consciousness flourishes, the wisdom is right in front of us, so simple and so clear. It is no secret. Souls in transition, we are all distracted, in varying degrees, looking to the other side for what lies just within our reach.

To become more luminous with every step (and every thought), however many the diversions the soul clings to, is simply the reason of existence. When you truly understand that—truly grasp that fundamental reality—the questions disappear. Enlightenment follows. You realize that all the answers lie within you, as they live within all of the Prime Creator's manifestations of consciousness—at every juncture in the heavens, within every blade of grass of your sweetest meadows.

In the illusory fields of the lower dimensions, which tear at transiting souls with their extreme polar oppositions, it is the nature of reality to exacerbate suffering in those densities by vexing the mind with expectation of what magnificence lies beyond the veil. You want to know what lies ahead: you must know how the movie ends. It is the nature of human consciousness, with all your innate intelligence, to skip over the details and get to the conclusion succinctly and to the point.

Yet, as you know, the beauty is in the details.

But if the great moments of our existence, scripted and designed by the higher consciousness of all souls, could be published as a Definitive Manual of Evolution, all souls might finally be free to simply cease the search and lie about, in some ubiquitous Garden of Eden, waiting for the rainbow. To know how it all unfolds: surely this would ease the burden of our passing through the fields of duality, the struggle, and the doubts.

Ah, but then where would the joy of existence lie? What would be the purpose of any of it? What would we gain from that knowledge, and what would we miss, careening through the story lines of lifetimes, of the magic that surrounds us all?

We join here with the voices presented to provide you with the insights you seek from us as part of your progress toward reaching that understanding and, as always, our love encircles you, serving wherever and whenever we can. You have help on so many levels, and you have love, woven so beautifully, through your light strings.

Let this time of Gaia's emergence be surrounded in the beauty of your own making—recognizing that where you are is where you intended to be and trusting, dear star seed, that where you intended to be is the perfection of your own mind, painting the canvas of life.

Lift your weary wings—and fly.

Know the moment, and make it perfect.

And trust that, despite the chaos and noise, all is in absolute harmony in the Cosmos of Soul.

SEVENTEEN

TRANSITIONING FROM DENSE BODY TO LIGHT BODY

From my understanding, there is probably only one way through this transition, and that is through the awakening of our light body or spiritual DNA. From what I was able to gather, the spiritual DNA is our blueprint for our life purpose and the divine potential of each soul.

Our current two-strand DNA is not able to adequately handle this multidimensional energy field that is coming in. This spiritual DNA is an energetic image of our physical DNA, and it is spiraling energetically in specific patterns unique to each soul. It seems that the only way to activate its potential is through the understanding and functions of certain glands, primarily the thymus gland—considered the seat of the soul—and the pineal and pituitary glands.

What interests me today is how the proper activation of those glands and their integration allows the production of soma, which is known as the divine hormone.

Could you talk more about soma?

Let us first comment that there is more than one way to activate the dormant DNA within you and that, with or without a deep understanding of the endocrine system and other chemical reactions within the brain and the mind, you are still capable of altering your light body through the focused will and the expanded, unconditional heart.

It is our experience that the greatest leaps in consciousness (and that most certainly would apply to the case of reactivating human DNA) are acquired through the psychic, intuitive mind rather than the analytical processes of the logical mind.

We understand soma to be your reference to the hormone produced naturally in the human endocrine system, of which the pineal gland is the master regulator of both physical and spiritual light entering the auric field and the physical body. Soma is a chemical secretion produced in the pineal gland and distributed to the areas of the brain that surround the protective well of fluids in which the pineal gland is sheltered. From there, it is carried along the neurotransmitters to the entire field of biologically interactive units of consciousness, which derive from it various degrees of light as it bathes the soul.

Therefore, we wish to distinguish between the pineal gland itself and the hormone that interests you, soma, which the pineal secretes, along with serotonin, in the human brain and is then passed along the neural pathways.

The pineal gland, known to your ascetics and spiritual seekers as the third eye, is just that: an actual, physical third eye, that one that actually looks out not upon the sensate world in which you navigate your physical experience but upon the light of Spirit and, via the soma secretions, communicates that light to the entire being.

Attainment of a perpetual state of higher awareness, whereby this Spirit Eye is activated, has been inhibited in Homo sapiens by the deactivation of ten strands of your original twelve-stranded DNA light bodies. This we have elaborated on in earlier works. The master gland, or Spirit

Eye, will be fully operative when the original twelve strands of DNA have been reactivated—a process that is beginning to occur for many of you at this time of your rapid spiritual and planetary evolution

The chemical essence of soma, secreted into the neuroreceptors, carries the memory of your fully activated, fully integrated light body awareness, which is imprinted upon the master cell within the pineal gland. When you meditate, pray, and love at the pure heart level, soma is produced in greater quantities, causing states of profound awareness, vision beyond the sensate realm, and hallucinatory experiences of ecstatic heights. It allows you to access parallel worlds and dimensions and to observe or interact with conscious entities of other realms.

The effect of these chemical secretions is accelerated by the neuroconductors, the synaptic connections, whereby the nervous system of your exquisite circuitry boards link from the pineal gland to the entire nervous and endocrine systems, creating various reactions in the physical and spiritual bodies that you may know as body validations of psychic insights.

Is it even possible for us to activate this gland at this point?

The process of activating the pineal gland is inextricably linked to the primary activation of the third light strand of DNA, creating triangulation at the cellular level. That process itself creates the neurological impulse within the pineal gland to produce a surge in the secretions of soma into the neural networks and heighten the spiritual light within the brain and body. However, it is also to be noted that masters and accomplished Spirit practitioners are capable of illumination of the pineal gland, soma hormone, and other ecstasy-producing chemicals from the higher light of the human mind through highly focused practices of meditative states, tantra, and devotion.

Would this hormone develop our internal power for transmutation from a two-strand helix toward our original twelve-strand DNA?

The temporary surge of soma within the brain (brought about in meditation, prayer, and tantric practices) combined with an exceptionally focused conscious mind and other practices most definitely accelerates the activation process. The superconductivity of the hormone, interacting with the inter/extra and intracellular waters, alters the electromagnetic capacity of each cell, allowing for the higher frequencies of Spirit light to create the sacred geometries within the body at the cellular, subatomic levels.

We remind you that toxins in your water and food supply, particularly fluoride, cause rapid calcification of the pineal gland and are significant inhibitors to the process of producing soma. It is for this reason that we suggest that you who seek such acceleration be extremely conscious of the crystallized chemical compounds that you ingest as food. And there is the water—which is filled with damaging substances that deter your process.

Of these, fluoride collects as a powdery residue in the gland—this is not in your highest interest. We leave you to imagine why it has been forced upon you in your drinking water and hygienic materials and suggest you examine it more closely.

Moreover, toxic thought patterns, which generate inharmonious energy streams, disrupt the output and flow of soma.

If so, how can we go about activating it?

At this point of Earth's evolutionary contribution to your sun's ascension, we perceive that the energies permeating the planet can assist you in anchoring up to six strands of DNA, material that lies within you, awaiting your conscious creation of the magnetic light pathways that will call DNA back into its original functioning energy matrix.

Whatever guidance is available to you now (and there are many masters proposing various methodologies) this activation process will happen only when you are intent upon releasing the shadow of your emotional bodies and silencing the ego self. It will happen when you are capable of focusing your minds to such a perfected extent that you can create, through the conscious intention, these light streams that will draw the displaced DNA material back to its original grid lines.

Full activation of the twelve-stranded DNA system, the Christ grid, will be potentiated at the time of your planetary ascension.

Is there a part of this awakening being done automatically because of the higher frequencies of the planet and the shift that is going on?

Yes, without question, Gaia—a conscious, living being—is experiencing the waves of photonic light in her own lighthouse center—the point of entry for the Spirit light, which is the brilliance beyond the physical light of Ra, your sun.

This powerful point of energy absorption, where the flow of galactic consciousness enters the Earth, is most acute at the Giza Plateau. Your sun, a living, brilliant celestial being, is receiving attunements from the cosmic rivers of photonic light entering your quadrant of the galaxy, and then this flow is filtered into the planets, which make up the body of Ra. It pours into Gaia at that particular location, as if the region is a magnetic conductor to the electric sun.

As that occurs, the Earth and the other planetary deities of your solar system are simultaneously receiving the heightened waves of evolutionary, shifting universal consciousness at all levels. It permeates your galactic environment. It flows through and within all living beings in these fields—both on the Earth and within the bodies of all stellar deities, whose light breeds abundant life.

How is this realignment affecting those people who are not conscious of the process?

Every unit of consciousness within the cosmos is linked to every other, whether it is aware of that oneness or whether it chooses to perpetuate a state of isolation and separation.

To be conscious of the process of your acceleration as a species—as Earth dwellers—is so very much more powerful and significant than your concerns about your individual progress and spiritual epiphanies.

For those of you who are dedicated to that end, the attainment of a higher purpose and understanding of the passage of so many life cycles for all living beings is, by nature of that awareness, conscious of the process of your global acceleration toward the dawn of the awakened human.

Those who are focused, instead, upon their own individual achievements, without regard for the greater body of consciousness, will still sense a quickening and may very well have moments of enlightenment. However, without being connected at the greater level, the moments remain fleeting, for it is the outpouring of unconditional love for *all beings* and the euphoria of that collective consciousness that illuminates the lighthouse of the soul.

There are yet others, who are intent upon pursuing the darker fields of human emotion. No amount of cosmic activity—no quantum of love and light—can alter the destiny of an individual who chooses suffering. These individuals have already determined that they intend to cling to the material world, to take from it as much as they can, and then to abandon it when they reach their completion on any given material plane. Even those who are in extreme suffering and lack—at some level that they do not understand—choose this destiny.

We remind you that this is occurring not only on your planetary body but also on others within your solar system.

Is it so that the activation of the light body at its completion will allow the Higher Self the possibility to download and permanently anchor the complete DNA/RNA grid that is composed of sixty-four distinct seals that are located inside all our chakras?

In the vastness of the multiverse of infinite possible realities, there is no completion point in the process of light body awakening. We never stop activating the light body—we continue refining our consciousness until we merge back to the godlight. It is a process that is as perennial as the flow of light through the cosmos, the soul climbing the spiral of light in its search to return to the source—the all that is.

Not even that moment of return is finite, for we exist as eternal light in that immeasurable brilliance.

What will be important now to all of you is that you achieve the understanding that your experience is never-ending—that there is no pinnacle to reach. These theorized measures of achievement and arrival are all illusory, reflections of the dimension in which you still hold resonance. To learn that each step is just as important and beautiful as the ones that you envision ahead of you is the true key to spiritual mastery.

If people miss the great moments of the journey, how will they recognize the point of arrival?

As for anchoring the DNA within you, know that you are capable of mastery in every moment of your existence in the physical realm in which you currently hold resonance and that all of the materials, codes, and information exist within you—*right now*.

With the currents of cosmic energy moving through your galactic sphere and the effect this is having on the intrusive electromagnetic grid that was thrown around your planet by invasive forces, the cosmic level is facilitating the acceleration of this process. This diminishing grid allows more Light Beings to get through, and this is occurring at many levels now (some of which you are aware, some of which are still undetectable to you).

Let us always remind you that in the free-will zone of your Earthly experience, it is you who determines the richness of your experience. Will you focus on what lies ahead of you, what you lack and desire, or will you celebrate each moment, the small and seemingly insignificant steps, as well as those giant leaps to which you so aspire?

In what dimension is a body able to do this? Would this involve the ascended masters?

You have the tools to begin the process of light body activation at this time. Given the intensity of Earth's polarized fields, however, we do not see the potential for reactivation of the twelve strands—Christ consciousness—until you are at the point of passing through the ascension cord.

This is a process that you will create within you when you have understood that *you* are the master, the sovereign Spirit, and the light. You will be assisted as well by the accelerated energy emissions of your planetary deity—Gaia.

Do you have anything more to add?

The process of activating the DNA begins with the assembly or reorganization of a third light filament. This can be achieved through a process of deep meditation and altered consciousness. Proper guides will help with this or, for those of you capable of extreme focus and auto-induced states of deep meditation, you can do it alone.

We have made materials available to you so that you may utilize our voice if you wish it.

Once the third strand is activated, creating immense energy in the pineal gland, triangulation (the sacred form upon which the rest of the DNA recovery will be based) is formed within the nuclei of all cellular units within your being.

The dynamic geometries of this triangulated DNA structure send charges of electromagnetic fields, something very similar to lightning, into the brain, perpetuating the activation of the pineal gland and the production of soma.

From my understanding of things, this planetary transition seems to be a divine intent brought about by a collective purpose, from the Universe and humanity, to accelerate the evolution of life and consciousness.

The reason behind this experience, among other things, is to correct a situation initiated in Atlantis thousand of years ago—an experience gone awry. Along with the Brotherhood of Light, the Sirians and the Pleiadians are key players. It seems that the job of the Pleiadians is to focus energy on the human heart, while the Sirians focus on the geometry of the physical body, the light body. We have to have both to be able to go from one dimension to the other.

Is this an accurate perception?

In the higher dimensions, where darkness fades and the light of Supreme Being shines through the haze of slowed frequencies, everything filters through the One Heart. It is the focus of all Light Beings to shine the unconditional love of source into the pure waters of the Cosmos of Soul—that universal flow of light and love that emanates from every heart and soul of the living. It is not limited to the experience of those resonating at the fifth density or dimension.

At our station in the fields of consciousness that you know as the sixth dimension, we are aware of the cosmometric proportions and dynamic numerological ratios between all things, all realities, all dimensions. Even in the darkness of other realms, there are patterns of recognizable, godly proportion. These exist in the most exquisite patterns of light refracting, reflecting through the dimensions, and shining through the density of the physical Universe.

All of this—the beauty, the love, and the light of the sacred codes of universal design—connects galaxies, Universes, all densities, all realities... however much the illusion of separation would veil it to the uninitiated.

We invite you to consider that the evolutionary events in your realm—the acceleration of which you speak—are, above all, a reflection of your solar deity's preparation for its release from the limitations of the physical Universe and not a correction of past karma.

It is important to recognize that Gaia is an aspect of your sun and that her process and yours are reflections of the solar deity's evolution.

Those who are observing Earth's awakening cannot resolve the karma that has been forged of past events and would not intend to intervene in that experience. We are participants in the celebration of Spirit climbing higher, and that includes the Spirit of Ra, your solar deity. We are watchers, reaching out to help guide those who seek it, but we are not intent upon correcting, judging, or resolving your own karmic creations.

We have learned from experience that even our gifts, intended to raise humankind from its limitations, inevitably turn against you in the hands of those who pursue their powers for control over you. That is why we have retired them from your realm, awaiting the peak of conscious awakening—a moment that follows this time of clearing and liberation.

Is it also accurate to say that the Sirians have created a different hologram for planet Earth—a context of reality enabling us to better understand what is taking place?

From our vantage point, we observe Earth and all the celestial bodies as living organisms, conscious beings with a very distinct and significant soul purpose to fulfill and make manifest.

Gaia, and other planetary deities that comprise your solar system, emit enormous fields of conscious energy that permeate the planetary environment and then interact and exchange with the congruent planets that enjoy your cosmic space.

We have not created illusory fields for you. Your planet, Gaia, is your teacher. Only one hologram of Sirian origin remains in the Earth codes, and that is the vortex in which we contain the thirteenth crystal skull of the days of Atlantis—soon to be revealed to humankind.

Those of you who are paying attention, listening to the *music*, are able to understand exactly what is happening. Those who are still sleeping, bowing to fear and the lower aspects of human emotion, have yet to understand how the process of breaking down your inoperative systems and releasing yourselves from your chains can be painful before you reach your liberation.

But reach it, you will.

EIGHTEEN

UNDERSTANDING OUR COUNTERPARTS IN SPIRIT

I was wondering about our soul family on the other side. Members of this soul family are in the hundreds or thousands, but we do have a core family, and they would be a much smaller group in which we choose to incarnate with lifetime after lifetime. With this group, we share knowledge and experiences while we build memory together. It is our real family, our celestial family, our divine family, and we have incarnated with them since we have been created as a soul. Today I would like to talk about our core family.

How do the experiences that we have here on Earth affect the core family, and where do these members of the core family come from? Do we, for example, all come from the same planet or Universe?

Collectives of souls are united not by their locations of origin but by their soul intentions. As the awakening beings are beginning to understand, through the evolving revelations of cosmic (as opposed to Earth-related) physics, Universes are reflections of each other, and you can—and often do—exist in simultaneous realities: parallel Universes, time lines, and dimensions.

As you walk through the lifetime you have selected to experience on Earth, you may very well be creating another outcome, a possible reality in another Universe or reality, which, by the nature of the reflective aspects of light moving through the endless cosmic sea, will be very similar to that reality—your Earthly life. You feel that you exist there and there alone, and yet you journey to these other realities all the time: when you sleep, when you meditate, when you daydream.

As all conscious beings travel the spiral of light, there are those (as you refer to as core family) that resonate with your soul's integrity of Spirit and the music it emanates, as it moves from the dense to the light. They may be just ahead of you, as are we for the human race, reaching out so that you might find guidance as you climb out of the darkness. They may be behind you, awaiting that loving hand that you will extend to the needy.

They may be human, like you, or they may be another species entirely. What binds you is the *music*—the vibration and the intention your soul has determined as your purpose to experience *I am* consciousness. What unites you is unconditional love.

The way I understand this is that not all members of our core family incarnate at the same time. Some stay on the other side and act has a support group. At this time, do some incarnate in places other than Earth, or is the experience being done mainly on Earth?

There is no precision to the question of simultaneous reality. You connect with these soul collectives throughout your physical lifetime and beyond. Know that when you pass from lifetime to lifetime in the process of reincarnation, you are assisted. When you rest, between lifetimes—there too you are guided by souls who resonate with your process. And as you can well imagine, at the time of a collective ascension, as you are about to experience, you will share the wonder with any number of souls who have determined that they would take part in the process, as you did—before you entered this lifetime.

As remote as it appears to you now, know that the other side is as close to you as is the air to the Dolphin Beings. They dance in and out of the ocean's waves, weaving their music into the currents, leaping at will into the beyond, and drawing that experience back into their song.

How are information and knowledge communicated between core family members? Is it during the sleep state?

They travel upon waves of consciousness that transcend time, location, and space. It is not limited to any particular wavelength upon which you are operating.

In the states you refer to as delta wave emission and theta frequencies, you have less stimulus at the conscious level to interfere with your mind's emissions, but, clearly, then too you are capable of sending and receiving thought and emotion through all dimensions.

Thought is the primordial impulse of universal frequencies. First there is the thought—the conscious intention. Then there is sound—the wave. The manifestation, whether in the physical realm or beyond, follows.

Can a soul family give solutions to problems of its members during their incarnation, or can this only come from themselves, their guides, or Higher Self?

Dear one, how we wish for all of you the understanding that no one can provide solutions to your obstacles, for they are the manifestations of your own belief systems! Every soul is the proprietor of every aspect of illusion and clarity. The search for happiness and illumination is facilitated when one comes to the realization that no one can adjust another's reality or find answers to what another perceives as problems.

Your creation of such disharmonies is part of your process at the soul level. In the material Universe, the soul is confronted with a significant amount of darkness—the absence or suppression of light. They are patterns you have created to learn the meaning of existence. You have a sovereign right and responsibility to alter these, at your desired pace, to allow more light to enter your heart.

Whether you define this as a Higher Self or you determine it to be an aspect of your consciousness as a physical being of the Earth, you are there to learn, in your passing, that you create all of it: the joy, the suffering, the letting go. All of it is the process of the soul climbing higher.

Your guides are there to help you recognize the bends and turns in your path—helping, but never interfering, with your journey of self-realization and awakening to the purity of unconditional love. You learn this by forgiving and embracing your obstructions, by forgiving and embracing others who appear to interfere in your pursuit of happiness and awakening, and by taking responsibility for all that occurs in that process.

As a celestial family, do we have a soul purpose?

The purpose of all beings is to climb the spiral of light and then to help others rise as well. Some intend to drink long and insatiably of the darkness of material pleasure, others to hasten the journey to know the brilliance of love unfolding. It is the common experience of all units of consciousness, from the mineral kingdom, where brilliant crystalline matrices reflect the intention to manifest beauty, to the most evolved species of your Earthly experience: the humans, the great whales, and the Dolphin Beings.

Your own personal experience gives you much insight into what level of awareness is shared by your collective.

Know that you coexist in the futuristic sense as you do in the past sense, and as you ascend the spiral, you will finally recognize how these are illusory aspects of your existence in the physical Universe.

If they are a support group, can we work with them in the same way as we work with guides?

More than a structure of support, the core family to which you refer is a collective of souls working from the same vibrational context as you are in this passing. Because you are not limited to what appears to you in your awake, logical mind as the time zone, you can and do move through diverse energy fields to connect with these like-minded souls.

Unlike your guides, who are in absolute service, the individuals of a core group of souls are working through realities similar to yours, and you glean truths from their experience as they do through yours. This occurs whether or not you consciously intend to make a connection with them, for they resonate at the same frequencies as you—whatever dimension, whatever location on the space-time continuum.

Of course, your conscious intention to connect with them opens channels of communication!

If all those who are reading these lines would put out the intention and do the work to communicate with their Higher Self or guides or soul family, how would this impact this grand experience? Would there be an acceleration in the whole process?

Just like the drop of water in the pond, the individual desire to work on higher planes creates a gentle ripple in the cosmic sea. The collective intention to raise consciousness from the fear and lack mind-set that grips you to the understanding of your greater purpose would create gigantic waves of light, moving through the Universe—bringing purification and resolution of so much of the disharmony that seems to attach itself to matter.

Would this have a consequence on the plan of the dark forces whose purpose is to keep us as long as possible from our galactic heritage?

When conscious beings no longer respond and react at the animal level of survival—in which your interaction with each other is self-serving, fear-based, and unyielding—the dark ones will have no means to control you. In the light of your One Heart, where you are community—selfless and heart-centered—nothing can deter you.

As to the intention of those who currently rule over the planet to somehow prevent you from partaking of the reunion, understand that they do know that the time of your orphanage is coming to a close and they cannot stop it. They are scrambling for methodologies to manage you when this becomes reality and the entire human race and animal kingdoms are welcomed into the greater family of conscious beings.

Your false leaders, determined to lower the vibrations of your world, can create the illusion of hopelessness and powerlessness among you only if you allow yourselves to believe the feast of lies being fed to you.

Those of you who are awakening know that no matter what comes to you in the 3-D landscape of illusion, you are on your way to a new dawn. You trust that you are on a higher path, guided by the light of your oversoul, and that you are eternal, beautiful, and free.

Wouldn't this communication be one of the single most important ways to end duality?

As long as you exist in the physical realm, you will experience duality in various measures. It is coded into your DNA with its dual aspects of electromagnetism. These polar aspects are necessary to the physical world, for they define it in so many ways. Without shades of darkness, you cannot see form—it cannot appear in a whiteout of pure light.

Imagine the rainbow, from which you draw so much inspiration and celebration. It appears where darkness meets light.

We believe your concern is with regard to the extreme polarity that currently dominates the human condition. At a time when the energy shifts in your galaxy are of such an extreme intensity, human Spirit is either thrown into despair and a manic sense of purposelessness or, like you, it sees ever so much more clearly, the path of Spirit.

You are refining that duality, but it doesn't end. . . . However, the arrival of extraterrestrial beings will most definitely serve as an enormous catalyst in the process through which you liberate yourselves from the extreme polarity of current events upon the Earth and that sense of separateness, detachment, and fear.

NINETEEN

THE CAPSTONE OF EGYPT

From what I've been able to gather here and there, it seems that there was a golden capstone of 5 feet thick and 28.2 feet in length on top of the Great Pyramid. It was originally white, and it acted as a focal point for energy connections throughout the Universe. It currently lies hidden in seven pieces throughout the Earth: one on each continent, hidden deeply in the Earth. One would be in Lac Louise, Canada, another around Lake Titicaca in Peru, one also near Ayer's Rock in Australia.

What is the correct information concerning the capstone?

We do not share this vision as you have described it, but we can confirm to you that a powerful electromagnetic conductor did originally adorn the Great Pyramid at Giza. It was comprised of oricalcum—not gold—the most exquisite and conductive ore to ever exist in the Earth realm, a mineral utilized in the creation of most of the Atlantean energy networks and temples.

This mineral was created at the time through an alchemical transmutation that has been lost to your contemporary society. It was a gift of forces beyond your world, teachers of the wisdom keepers of Atlantis, who foresaw the Golden Age of man returning, so many thousands of years hence, to your planet. That Age of Enlightenment was marked by the building of the Great Pyramid.

Beneath this structure were placed several laser crystals, which were positioned at different angles, like the so-called shafts in the pyramid structure, to align with different star systems.

The oricalcum cap and the crystal matrix served to refine the cosmic flow of energies entering Earth at the Giza area into energy streams that could be utilized to hold Gaia's entire energy grid in balance and to illuminate the inner world of Agharta.

What kind of information is encrypted on this capstone? Is it hidden in one piece or seven pieces?

It is not hidden in pieces around the Earth. It was deliberately disintegrated many thousands of years ago, as it was determined by the Galactic Federation to be too powerful a technology for a world that had declined into chaos and the violent solution in the last days of Atlantis.

If you wonder if this device will return to Earth: no, it will not. It was of another day and reality. Look beyond the gold and glitter and know that the pyramid still retains all the power and glory. It is now more in tune with the level of pervading human consciousness.

What you didn't know is that at the moment that marked the millennium in your time reference, an attempt to place a model of this device was thwarted by celestial forces dominated by the Sirian star, Sothis, which was directly aligned with the pyramid at that time.

With the activation of Giza that is taking place, how is it affecting the planet at this time and also you on Sirius? I am sure that we do not realize the importance of this activation not only for the Earth and its humanity but for the entire Universe.

This location of Earth's geophysical body is the entry point for the cosmic flow of conscious energy that enters the planet. Therefore, it is always "activated."

The conscious intention of so many elevated human beings, drawn to and into the pyramid, interacts with the crystalline matrix of the granite inner being of the structure, where the memory of the device is still held.

This memory can only be retrieved through the purified heart. When lower vibrations seek to tap the flow or to direct it for purposes other than the highest good of all beings, they are thwarted.

TWENTY

FIRST CONTACT

What a confusing thing this whole concept is. I think that we really do need to understand what is happening on that level. A lot of people are confused at this point and do not know what to believe.

One topic intrigues me, and I have wondered about it for a while: Because we have trouble making first contact with ourselves, it seems somewhat odd to me to expect that you—our brothers and sisters from the other side of the veil—will make contact with us. But on the other hand, I really think that our desire to reestablish this cosmic connection is very genuine. We really want to have these contacts with our sisters and brothers from the other side of the veil.

In your book Atlantis Rising, *you say at the end: "Contact is eminent." What do you mean exactly?*

Contact with the galactic family of beings within your own solar system—physical beings—is about to occur at the global level.

It already has at the governmental level, but the government is intent upon keeping the population in the dark about what is so clearly and boldly occurring right in front of you, within your field of vision.

Daily now, crafts fly through your atmosphere and into your sunny skies, just as they appear as strange lights in the night. They appear and hover over cities, mountains, fields, and lakes. This activity is intended to orient you and prepare you for final contact, when this presence will make itself known—without doubt, without room for denial—to the entire population.

Know that within your solar body, all life-bearing planets are interactive, enjoying the exchange of commerce, technology, and resources. Only Earth (and let us refine that to mean the majority of human beings on your planet) remains in that state of detachment from the greater family—the galactic community.

Those in power are fully aware of extraterrestrial life and the activities under way to prepare you, the orphans of your galaxy, for the revelation. They have been given a mandate to either reveal their knowledge and hidden archives or to step aside, to allow the new vision to seed within you.

It is imminent, a necessary key to your ascension, for you are as much a part of this greater family as you are children of Gaia and they of other worlds nearby.

We stress the importance of your preparation for this event as the key to its outcome. Currently, you are viewed as a violent, warring species—a danger to all who dare to approach you. War appears to be your first recourse to conflict, a sign of a self-extinguishing society. As a whole, you destroy your resources and habitat with waste, rage, and disregard for all life. Your weaponry has now made you a threat to harmonious planets that occupy your same space in the galaxy.

The councils of peaceful planets are united in the search for a way to greet you—to enter your sphere—without creating massive panic and fear and without instigating that same warlike response.

The overriding intention is to provide you with the knowledge of more advanced societies and higher sociological frameworks so that you can experience a wave of greater meaning to life than that which pervades in your world.

There are many of you now working furiously to raise the vibration of your world, and it is through you and to you that we, beings of other dimensions, are able to make contact. You are the ambassadors of the Galactic Federation every bit as much as those who will appear to you—because you are intent upon drawing more light into the hearts and minds of the suffering, the fearful, and the misguided.

What does first contact mean for us? Do we need to make first contact with ourselves before we can do it with another race or Light Being? Are we still just looking for help from the outside instead or looking inside ourselves?

Entertaining the possibility of interplanetary communication does not necessarily indicate the disempowered mind of one seeking a savior. It is a vital part of your passage as you rise to the incredible awareness of limitless intelligence within the Universe and humankind's part in that greater community.

Clearly, the arrival of thousands of crafts in your skies and their communications for the entire world of human beings will dramatically affect some of the most primitive behaviors, as it will the intelligentsia.

All of you will be confronted with a new paradigm, something you are moving toward with great rapidity, as you see the old one crumbling all around you. This process of breaking down the structures that have held you in a state of oblivion, however frightening they appear to you now, are essential to your preparation for what comes next: your peaceful coexistence with other civilizations and your joint passage to a lighter, more refined dimensional frequency.

Know that it has everything to do with you. We are only observers of your play, one we have lived through ourselves. At times, we have intervened, hoping to assist you. We have learned from that, and now we only participate, as best we can, as guides—offering you a vision of what love can create. Dear ones, it is all about moving from the darkness to the light. It is not complicated. It is the way of all conscious beings. You cannot reach it through the logical mind. It is through the heart that you can feel and embrace it.

TWENTY-ONE

THE DARKER SIDE OF HUMANITY AND THE INFLUENCE OF THE DARK FORCES

I think that the biggest hurdle to a smooth transition is how humanity is deeply into the victim consciousness, far from the consciousness of who they really are. I think that this prevents us from taking responsibility for everything that is happening. People are pointing their fingers at everybody else without taking responsibility for their participation in the situation that has been created. Of course, there is disinformation and manipulation of the masses, but humanity as a whole accepts giving control over to the media, the government, etc.

On the other hand, we all know that there are dark energies controlling a big part of the chaos right now. They want us to believe that it is impossible to get out of our situation, keeping us in the drama. The intention is to keep people as far as possible from the potential of freedom, totally involved in the illusion of lack on all levels—basically keeping us in a mode of competition instead of cooperation.

When I look at cities like Cairo, Mumbai, Calcutta, Lima, where extreme poverty is overwhelming, where pollution and chaos seem to be a way of life, where everyone is trying to survive, I say to myself: Martine, how can people be in such misery and then try to eliminate it? It seems impossible to do, but how can this continue? I felt the fear in the air and saw how difficult it must be for them. It was overwhelming for me at the beginning, but then I realized that we are all responsible for this creation.

How can these big cities survive in the future?

In the cyclical nature of life, there are ups and down, comings and goings, ins and outs across the realms of all experience.

In more progressive worlds, conscious beings have learned to cohabitate their environment with respect for all forms of life—aware that the ecosystems are what nourish them, just as they are aware that without biodiversity all are extinguished.

Overpopulated urban areas, such as you describe, are inevitably doomed to fail as models for harmonious living, as they are utterly indifferent to the natural flow of energies and they exacerbate the unbearable living conditions of disorder, disharmony, and abuse.

Were you not at the point of solar ascension, we would suggest that such urban congestions upon the planet would not survive. However, as we do perceive your proximate passage to the next dimension, we suggest that this is not a reality that will play out in a future context.

Is there a way out for these people?

As people migrate to these urban mega-stations at a certain time, so do they eventually desire to return to more natural environments. Every individual is free to make such decisions in the free-will zone in which you reside. But do not resign yourself to the idea that the global condition is irreversible.

Are these places the stronghold of influence of the dark forces or the secret government?

Their stronghold is in the emotional waters of human consciousness, where they have managed to float horrific images of shadow and violence among the unawakened, frightening them into obedience and submission. Without your fear and resignation, they have no hold over you.

The Secret Government of which we have spoken for so long now has one intention and one alone—to lower the vibrational frequencies of Earth to a point that the planet Nebiru, the Secret Government's homeland, can entrain itself to those emissions and manage to be pulled into the ascension cord of your sun, along with the other planetary bodies in your solar system.

How are they coping with the fact that they are losing their battle?

They are revealing themselves, unwillingly, through their acts. They are desperate despots, recognizing that no matter how tightly they squeeze you, they can slow you down ... but they cannot control you. The more they exert their force, the more of you awaken to the truth. This is the absolute opposite of what they need in order to reel in their wandering planet.

Who, at this point, inside the Galactic Federation, is coping with them?

All interactive councils for harmonious relations among planetary biocenters are observing the activities of your shadow government. This is one of the most significant reasons for imminent arrival.

As we have told you before, intervention is only possible at that point where your activities of destruction affect life beyond your atmosphere. That has become an imminent threat, as you currently possess enough thermonuclear force to interfere not only with your sun's ascension but with other celestial families in your corner of the galaxy.

TWENTY-TWO

KARMA AS INFORMATION FOR THE GRAND EXPERIMENT

I would like to discuss not how karma is lived by humanity but rather how the Universe utilizes this information to progress.

Would it be fair to say that, for many of us, the work is more about giving information back to the Universe on this experience that is being lived? I think that being in the physical, we automatically create karma, but this karma is transmuted now into information. Through our actions, we participate in the blossoming of the experience of what is happening on Earth so the rising of consciousness can be recorded.

Is this perception accurate?

As immense as it will appear to you, attempting to understand it from the 3-D perspective, we propose that all thought, all intention, all energy, and all experience are recorded in the Cosmos of Soul.

When, for example, a negative event occurs in an individual or common experience, it plays out across the waves of the cosmos at a vibratory rate that affects the entire field of all existence. No matter how minute, no matter how immense, each wave remains in the sea of universal mind.

This information is chronicled in the universal record, where it resonates at a lower frequency and where, to those who contribute to its creation, it clings energetically to their soul's vibration. That is why and how one returns to it, lifetime after lifetime, for it is a vibration that holds the soul in a field of disharmony—that which the soul, seeking the highest truth, eventually resolves by what you call resolving karma.

The same holds true for actions and thoughts of the noble, higher mind. They resonate at a much higher frequency, traveling greater distances across the cosmic waves, and they carry more light, which shines through the fields of universal experience.

This source of conscious, light-filled information generates resonant fields of awareness in other realities and dimensions.

That is how we reach you.

TWENTY-THREE

ANSWERS FOR THE LIGHTWORKERS

For as long as there has been a New Age movement, there has been financial difficulty, deprivation among those who walk the spiritual path. I know that many people who chose to leave well-paying jobs to follow their calling and the promise of greater rewards now find themselves impoverished and unable to fulfill their soul's destiny and rather experience the ever-diminishing ability to manifest money.

It has been said in many messages, "Take a leap of faith and you will be rewarded. Do the first mile and we will do the rest." But for many it didn't happen, and they lost faith not only in the possibility of pursuing their calling but also in the messages. I know many Lightworkers who have abandoned the desire to pursue their dream.

Is this happening because, at the cellular level, they have a belief that says: "If it is spiritual, it should be free"?

The reasons for such outcomes can be varied. Many individuals, positioned as spiritual leaders and guides, are still not clear of their own demons and fears and therefore cannot be of service to others. They are not in their highest truth, and are shut down because of their compromised intentions. In other cases, where their core belief is that they do not deserve abundance, it will not be made manifest simply because they decide to take on the activity of spiritual pursuits and practices.

The tests of the true Spirit warrior are many. Indeed, they never end. Some yield to the obstacles and obstruction, and others rise to the challenge. To lose faith in a dream is to lose trust in your own ability and purpose.

We do remind you, however, that doing the first mile, as you say, does not mean that an external force will do the rest. Perhaps it is here, in the mind-set of disempowerment, that such individuals give in to their fear.

The art of manifestation is not outside of you—it is within every thought that you project into the ethers. It is you who creates your reality, and most likely the leap of faith is only one of many steps you must take to live your truth, to walk in the light of your heart, and to create abundance in your life mission.

One of the places that we hear this over and over again is in our religions. Service to others should be free, and service to self alone is selfish! What is so surprising to me is everybody knows that one of the most affluent institutions is the religious one. Just that should tell us how inappropriate a belief that is.

Even today, with the acceleration of energy, it seems as difficult for many as it has always been, particularly for healers.

That is indeed entertaining if you consider that most religions on your Earth are organized in such a way as to create endless flows of revenue into their secret coffers. Perhaps all those trapped in such a belief system might consider that the resistance of religious organizations to the spirit movement is based on their intention that you not interfere with their collection of resources from the obedient observers of their doctrines.

If money is utilized to propel your work for Spirit to the greater community, to serve the light, to help make your world a field of light, then it can only be celebrated as the energy you need to move forward. You share this source with others so that it is flowing through you to those of your communities, and all benefit.

It is greed, or a sense of unworthiness, that breaks the flow—not the flow itself—that shuts down the failed spiritual practitioner.

Is it that some of the gifts are not meant to make a living out of them? The same thing as not every channel has information that has to be published?

Only those bestowed with a gift can determine whether or not it is timely and appropriate to share it with the world, but those individuals will be tested for purity of intent before the doors open and they are enabled to give and be received.

The false prophets and magicians will eventually be revealed and disabled. It is our experience that those chosen to serve as instruments for light, beings intent upon assisting the human race, are most definitely given the information to be shared—not to be held for their personal advantage. But they have to be willing to serve and be clear messengers of the light.

Judgment of such individuals, many of whom dedicate their lives to the pursuit of wisdom, is a reflection of fear and lack. What is most important is that you support the work of anyone who is genuinely concerned with raising the collective consciousness. Theirs is not an easy task, and it requires focus, determination, and, in many instances, self-sacrifice.

Unfortunately, not all those channels are working with Light Beings. Many have connected to astral entities with less-than-pure intentions. That is why we invite you to scrutinize what comes into your awareness and to use discernment with all information now being made available.

Is it about finding balance between the service to self and service to others?

Honoring the self is not necessarily being in service to self. To serve as a spiritual teacher or healer, one must stand for truth and the highest intention, in service to the betterment of the all, still honoring his or her own being.

When will the energy support all Lightworkers in realizing their calling and living their passion?

When they have focused their intention upon the highest good of the entirety, when they are pure of intention and selfless in service, when they recognize that they create the energy through the frequencies they send into the cosmic sea.

TWENTY-FOUR

TOOLS FOR ATTUNEMENT

In your book The Cosmos of Soul, *you say: "... for, as you are being re-coded to assimilate the third strand, you are reliving as memory the past life scenarios of your many incarnations in the Earth realm. This is occurring now to facilitate your pulling up from the subconscious all the layers of your being that, as evolutionary triggers, have brought you to this moment."*

This has been occurring to me in recent years, but what I would like to discuss today is another experience of attunement.

In January 2009, in a workshop in Egypt with Patricia, at one point we were led in a meditation. I must say that this meditation was quite powerful. In fact, it was one of the most powerful meditations I've ever had. It was the first time I really felt that I left to go somewhere. But what was more fascinating to me was that at the beginning of the meditation, I saw an Indigo screen come down, as opposed to the white screen that I usually see. At first I said to myself: "I won't see anything on a blue screen!" But then I saw these beautiful luminous white symbols or geometric figures come one after the other. This lasted for a while, and I remember being so grateful for seeing this. Then I don't remember anything else except Patricia trying to get us out of the meditation. At first when I came out, I thought, "Wow, that was short," but then Patricia told us that we were "gone" for ninety minutes!

What was this blue screen with the luminous symbols? Were the symbols codes, a language, a message?

We exist on the blue ray. It is a background through which we are able to perceive the light forms of all beings resonating at this density.

You were consciously connecting to our realm, and those messages—appearing to you as symbols—are representative of the cosmometric designs and sacred proportions that define our environment (just as they define yours!).

At this level of consciousness, we absorb light through patterns of conscious design, aware of Prime Creator's flawless beauty, through which the flow of all energy is made manifest.

Do you recognize how, in the right circumstances and with the right mind and intention, you can experience your own multidimensionality?

Was it work being done on my DNA?

It was you, sweet soul, soaring beyond limitation: believing, intuiting, knowing that you are capable of absorbing unlimited light and also of rewiring your circuitry to anchor that light within you.

Was this done by the High Council?

We worked through our channel, Trydjya, to take you farther than you may have traveled before, in the process of directing a third light beam into the existing double helix—to which the relevant bits of DNA/RNA are magnetically attracted and take form as a third strand of DNA.

This was my experience, but I am sure that the other participants felt a sort of soaring in this meditation. Can you explain what happened in general? I'm sure that everybody had some sort of experience.

In that moment of commitment among all present, when each determined to initiate the process of DNA activation, we did observe activation within all of you. This we experience as light exploding from your pineal gland into the ethers, just as it sends the electric current through every cell of your bodies.

It is always a magnificent moment to behold when conscious beings commit to accelerating their process, and we are honored to serve you in this capacity.

And what about crop circles? Are they one of the most powerful places to be right now? Because the crop circles change every year, is the energy renewed also?

The crop formations, as you no doubt understand, are interdimensional in nature. That is to say that it is consciousness from higher dimensions, manifesting sacred forms within your fields of experience.

We, Sirians of the sixth dimension, do actively partake in this form of communication with those of you whose hearts and minds are open to receiving us. We are joined by Light Beings of other frames who also hold the intention to reach you.

When you enter these formations, our temporary temples, you experience another worldly presence, which is your

Spirit shifting into another context of reality—even if only for a moment.

With each season, new designs are imprinted on the fields, reflections of our desire to awaken within you the ability to read the cosmometry of all creation.

Where would you recommend for us to go for higher attunement?

We suggest you take yourselves to the power centers of Gaia with the intention not only to receive but to give. Shifting from the desire to receive—to get something—and into an awareness of what your love and devotion can create is the purpose, truly, of interacting with the sacred centers of your planetary deity.

However, as well you know, it is never necessary to physically enter a space. You can be there in your astral form—you can be there in your mind.

Follow your heart. It leads you through all experience on the space-time continuum of your physical journey, while the soul acquires experience from that process for the journey beyond.

TWENTY-FIVE

THE MYSTERY OF DIMENSIONS

What a mystery the concept of dimensions still is. We all want to be in the fifth, but we surely have a lot of trouble doing the work to get there. Many think that it is as simple as going with the flow... the energy will automatically bring us to its door. Others still think that it is like a fuzzy wall of fog that we need to cross by 2012.

I understand that in 2012 we will be entering a higher version of the fourth dimension that is about balance and harmony—not the fifth—and that we will be in the fourth dimension for about eighty years.

But I ask you, how is that possible if dimensions are not measured by distance or time... everything is lived at the same time? Who is in the fourth dimension—the Earth, humanity?

Why, we ask you, do you all want to be in the fifth dimension? Is this the expression of an expectation that has been created within you from an outside source?

Yes!

Believing this limits your joy at your present station, just as it limits your potential to leap past that phase completely.

For your understanding, the fourth dimension is a sort of clearing station for souls ascending the spiral of light—a place where a giant leap from material consciousness brings the soul to the understanding of how all reality is one's own creation.

As time does not exist there, we are curious about your precision with regard to the time span (a linear construct) of eighty years. This pursuit of specific definitions of a future existence, from the 3-D perspective of linear time, is, again, a reflection of your current sense of limitation. It is not at all representative of the unlimited potential with which you will be presented in what you call the fourth dimension, if not the possibility that you sabotage your own journey through a sort of predetermined design of your desired outcome.

When your solar deity ascends to this dimension, all beings in the solar body that have elected (from the field of possible realities) to ascend, rather than to return to the wheel of incarnation, will find themselves in the no-time of four-dimensional consciousness. From there, each individual soul essence will determine its next station—or density—of conscious existence.

At the fourth level, one still retains body consciousness, and for many this is still so very important. The identity of the body temple is still intact, and the connection with the previous physical lifetime is still very dominant in the individual.

You can understand why we tell you that, at first, you may not even recognize that you have made the shift. At the moment your sun passes through the ascension cord, your entire solar body will find itself just outside of the material realm, resonating to a lighter, higher field of consciousness.

There will be great cataclysms, more of what you are experiencing now, before the passing. Those who find themselves in these disaster areas decided, well before they incarnated on your planet, that they intended to spend far more time on the wheel of reincarnation. As difficult as it is for you to embrace such an idea, we ask you to consider and remember that the soul chooses the time and location it enters... just as it decides the time and location of its departure.

Those committed to the sensate experience will reincarnate again, at another place in the Universe of matter, to continue the process of learning. Those of you who came, instead, to be part of the ascension of your star will be carried along, into the next level of awareness.

From there, your spiritual development and your ability to hold the light will determine which vibratory signature (dimension) you will proceed to.

In my point of view, each dimension brings about a superior degree of consciousness. Dimensions are not separated by distance. Our belief system is the one putting distance between dimensions. They overlap each other but are accessible to everyone. It is not out there but inside us, always has been. We have to believe that it is possible for each one of us to experience the fifth dimension in our daily lives.

It is a vibration that will fuel our light instead of our density. When I think of the fifth, I see the words grace, refinement, enlightenment, *and* service. *We will no longer react to drama in the same way, creativity will be much more present, life in general will be less complex, and service to others will be our main goal. Going from one dimension to the next is done very gently—we will just feel very differently about things, and we will always be in contact with our Higher Self.*

Having said that, I don't think that the problems of the world still in the third dimension will simply disappear because we are living within the next dimension. We are just passing from the third to the fourth to the fifth—not to the tenth dimension. I do think that we will still witness wars, hunger in the world, corruption in the economy, but our reactions to them will be very different.

Challenges will happen, but we will deal with them differently. It is not a safe house for those who have lived a difficult life... a reward for good deeds either. We can only get there if we work on ourselves through the qualities of the heart and understand what real compassion means.

Is this statement somewhat accurate?

It is not the case that you automatically pass from one dimension to the next sequentially. Again, this is a linear concept, which is a reflection of your current reality—but not of the higher realms.

It is a matter of how much light an individual can anchor and what frequencies emanate from his or her conscious energy fields. All reality is about frequency and the soul's ability to adjust to and anchor differing quanta of light.

If you seek out and find pleasure from the material world, where density of matter slows the frequency of consciousness and clings to darkness, then you will continue upon the wheel of reincarnation, wherever that may take you in the physical realm of countless possibilities, and you will vibrate at the slowed pace of that realm.

In the case of your solar system, a great leap occurs, for a huge proportion of souls incarnate at the same time and location on the space-time continuum. The planet ascends to the fourth dimension, where time no longer governs the rhythms and pulse of the planetary deity and the living beings that dwell upon it.

The next level of light, or what you call the fourth dimension, is a springboard from which you are free to leap to other experiences, as will be determined by your individual and collective energy fields. As in the case of our process of ascension, there was such harmonious interaction among the beings of our solar family that we found we had barely shifted to the fourth dimension when we were suddenly so surrounded by the light that we could not hold on to the vibrational sequences at the fourth level. We found ourselves imbued in such bright light that our body consciousness disappeared almost immediately.

If we speak so often of how very important it is to shift your focus from your individual experience to that of the community, it is for this reason, reflected in the experience we have described. The more souls in transit focused upon the greater good of the all, the greater your capacity to anchor the light.

Also, in your leap away from the third dimension, you are progressed into a reality where your concept of past, present, and future is replaced with the conscious experience of simultaneous time. It is an enormous leap in consciousness—perhaps the greatest of all.

In the higher realms, you lose this sense of desired outcomes and the need for higher achievement, and you simply celebrate the passage.

Because you are in the six dimension, what is the difference between the fifth and the sixth? How did you live in the fifth?

We have never existed at the fifth dimension, so we cannot speak of it. The body of beings of Satais, entirely, found itself at the sixth dimension since our ascension. Many have proceeded to other fields; many of us have remained, as light-bodied guardians of this dimension, in service to all that pass here.

Is everyone on Sirius living in the same dimension at this point?

There are three stars in the Sirius system. Sirius A, Sothis, still remains in the physical Universe. It is currently without conscious life due to the complex galactic forces that surround it. Sirius B, Satais, has progressed to the sixth dimension in its entirety. Sirius C, Anu, still holds consciousness in the fourth dimension.

As for what is beyond us, let's just say that we know that it is unquestionably such an immense measure of light and love that, at our current level of consciousness, it is simply inconceivable. And yet, we trust that if it is our destiny to reach such frequencies, it will be very near to the moment that we approach the Godlight.

At this point of our existence, we exist to celebrate the light and to serve those who are moving toward it.

Just know that what truly matters is the ability to love what is before you—right now. Projecting ahead of you—to what will be—only disturbs the joy of what is. In a certain sense, it is utterly self-defeating, as it has you always chasing the rainbow while the light shines down upon you.

TWENTY-SIX

WHAT IS THE REAL NATURE OF HOPE?

Lately I was wondering about the concept of hope. On one hand, for millions of people on the planet, if they did not have hope for a better life, they would not have the will to survive or continue to strive for a better future—for themselves and for their children. From my observations, when we take away hope from a person or a group of people, despair takes place and some form of violence usually erupts while faith is completely cut off. So in this manner, hope offers better possibilities.

On the other hand, hope can take us out of the moment. We want things to be different than they are; we don't like what is in the now. We give power to the future rather than the present, hoping for something exterior to change things. In that manner, hope has no real value.

Faith, on the other hand, is the knowing that everything is perfect in this moment. It is surrendering to a higher force. But what about those who do not have faith, who do not understand about these spiritual concepts? From what I've seen, everybody understands hope. There is no discussion about it, while faith brings about many discussions. Is it real? Who has it? What does it take to have it? But it is very difficult to tell someone when they can barely feed themselves or are suffering violence through war or any other manner that the present moment is all there is and it is perfect.

Isn't hope really a form of faith or trust?

What is faith? It is the child of trust, and trust is the outcome of one's absolute knowing, as you state, at the quintessential core level of consciousness, that all is in divine order and that all life is eternal.

Hope is less empowered than faith, which is unconditional. It speaks of wanting to believe, whereas faith believes unequivocally.

What does it take, you ask, to have faith? To know that you do not die is the basis of it—to master the fear of your mortality. To believe that you choose your own destiny, just as the suffering have chosen theirs, is yet another significant foundation upon which faith holds ground.

Of course, the suffering will not hear the message that the present moment is all there is. In their existence of misery and pain, their only vision is to escape the moment. In victim consciousness, it is most difficult to embrace the understanding of how you create your own misery. Often these creations were formed in other lifetimes—or shall we say *realities*—and these often are veiled to the memory and the present vision.

If you can assist others in doing that so that they can be freed enough from the suffering to be able to reach a point where they are able to look at it, then perhaps you can speak to them of such concepts. But to help others, those who are victims of their condition or their own self-inflicted suffering, you will first need to relieve some of the intensity of their pain before you can reach them on an intellectual and spiritual plane.

I really do think that we, the people, can change things and make a huge difference in the world—women in particular, because of our kind nature.

Every time you touch someone, you give God hands. When you speak, you are capable of giving a voice to the light. Do you trust in your own divinity? Do you remember that you are a spark of that light? If so, you have faith that you can move mountains, and move them you will.

If not, you will settle for *trying* to manifest change. The trying, while valiant, is more a possible reality than the result of those who know, from the deep inner core, that they *will* manifest change.

All is determined by your own understanding of your godliness. Trust and go. Shine the light where you see darkness. Let your heart know no conditions of your intention to help others, affecting change.

TWENTY-SEVEN

LAST THOUGHTS ON 2010

What will be the most important change that you see coming in the year 2010, and how can we work the potentials of that year?

We see you tearing down the structures through which the global forces that wish to rule you have managed to keep you categorized and separated in classes, race, and religions. As fearful as many of you have become in this time of dramatic change, all are beginning to recognize how life upon your Earth will never be the same again.

Those comfort zones in which many of you have lived, in many ways anaesthetized to the suffering of so many beings that share the planet with you, are narrowing. As the walls of convention begin to crumble, the collective is becoming aware of the great changes that define Gaia's transformation as she prepares to leave the third dimension for higher ground.

Consider the difficulties you encounter when you make life choices that involve changes in your personal living environments, work, and relationships, and then ask yourself what it takes to make those giant leaps on the evolutionary spiral of cosmic proportions.

This is your reality at this point of departure—2010. You break down the old, move through the suffering, and begin to construct a new paradigm: redefining and refining the structures of extreme duality that have held you in separation, unifying the human race with other species of your planet, rebuilding a world that is in need of a higher level of compassion and conscious intent.

We tell you: be the change, the consciousness, and the compassion that you want for the world—for yourself, your loved ones, and for all those who seem to be remote and separated from you. By being constant, steady light through your wisdom, your egoless service, and your unconditional hearts.

From what you see, where will the greatest change occur? Will it be science, technology, medicine, the environment? All of the above?

All are interconnected. The most significant changes, however, are in humankind's perception of reality, as it mutates from what you have known to what you can create as a collective. As you become more attuned to the Earth, you recognize how the environment is a sterile description of Gaia's emotional experience. The more it is abused, the more she reacts, determined to release herself from the disharmonies perpetrated, predominantly, by your species.

You realize how all the tools you have to enhance your existence have been, to a very large extent, used to reduce the natural flow. Faced with your rapidly deteriorating ecosystems, these fields (science, technology, and medicine) will be shifting toward resolving the planetary imbalances—through love for the Earth rather than through the blind destruction that has marked your latest years.

Is 2012 still a marker, or did that potential also change?

Your expectations for any time-determined outcome always affect the time, which is only a point of reference in *your* dimension. Yet we do acknowledge that this significant point on the space-time continuum, the framework of the third dimension, marks the final phase of your preparation for passage.

From your side, what do you wish that by the year 2010 we will have accomplished?

That you learn to trust that, no matter where you are in time and space, you are always where you are meant to be and that you are guided… every step of the way.

TWENTY-EIGHT

FOR THE HIGH COUNCIL

As I am finishing my questions for you tonight, I cannot help but to feel grateful to a group of Light Beings that has been working with us for thousands of years. Even if we don't remember everything at this point, I want you all to know how grateful we all are for your presence, your love, and your patience to bring humanity back home. I know we have all traveled together at one point, I know that we will do it again, and it will be a grand moment for all of us.

Everyone in the Universe seems to be concentrating on us, on what is going on here on Earth, because of the Great Shift. Everybody is working so hard for us that it seems that we forget to express our gratitude to you on the other side. I know in my essence that you are not separate from us; you are our family, which we left so long ago to participate in this grand experience.

Many nights I wish that I could simply ask you, "How are you?" I wish you could tell me about Sirius and your life, about your work and if everything is going according to plan. I wish today that we could be together. . . .

Child of beauty and light, we are you and you are us. We are all sparks of divine light, souls of the *I am* awareness, moving upon the brilliant spiral that returns us to the infinite brilliance.

Know that no one is left behind. That mental construct of separation is an illusion of the realm of matter, where most still cannot see through the veil. All are exquisitely, divinely progressing at the pace each soul set for itself, when it leaped into the dark night of ignorance and began its climb back to the light.

We have known this journey—at a moment that once appeared to us as the past but that we now understand is the forever. We have known the darkness, the shadow, the extreme duality, its resolution... and we are now in a state of serving those who are coming out of those spheres of obfuscation.

Despite your concerns for your world and the disruptions that are defining Gaia's evolutionary progression, manifesting as fields of disharmony and suffering, you are right on track, swimming in the open seas of probabilities of your own creation, readying yourselves for what is to come. Always remember, however, that it is important, so important, that you celebrate what has been laid at your feet, just as much as you dream about what lies ahead or mourn what has gone before.

As elders to your experience, we wish for you a process no less splendid than ours, in which we have known the magnificence of our own stellar deity transcending the physical to the higher realms.

However, like you, we have had to face ourselves—confronting our personal and collective karma, moving through all the doubt and fear and anticipation on our own. This is the road we chose as individuals and as a collective of beings from the Sirian star Satais that once shined through the density of the material Universe. It is the way of all conscious beings: from the bright light to the darkness and then the deliberate and constant return.

Like many of you, we waited and hoped for assistance from other worlds, other realities, and, like you, we worried—for naught. What we learned was that the passing is no less significant, no less breathtaking than the arriving. This, beloved, is the greatest achievement of all—so simple, yet so difficult to grasp from the shadow lands of duality.

So often we ponder how we can comfort you, aware that your decisions to suffer or celebrate your shifting reality are aspects of how you perceive your own existence in the realm you know as your Earthly lives.

We ask you to imagine a glorious red rose, symbol of cultivated intention, where, in essence, humankind and seed make a contract to bring beauty into the world. Inherent in the consciousness of the seed is the potential: *I can be brought to perfection with your nourishment and love.* You, the conscious gardener, create as best you can an environment most suited for the desired outcome, and the seed, carrier of the codes of intelligence that construct that outcome, receives your expressions of love and guardianship. In its natural state of existence, it is coded with all the wisdom required for it to reach its full potential, which is the nature of all life. Such is the godly gift of our unique and collective design. You nurture the seed with all the elements it needs to thrive, and you wait, patiently, for the bloom. The warmth of the sun in springtime signals the soil to nourish the seed. Birds sing the music of renewal, and those sweet vibrations coax the bud to blossom. One day—that moment of manifestation—the ability and the awareness to celebrate that beauty, that intention, that explosion of life opens within your heart.

We ask you: Where do you focus the lens of your mind? Do you linger in a field of diminishing returns, wondering why only that one seed has come to flower, whereas others have yet to yield at your level of expectation? Do you project yourself into a sense of future, knowing that there will be more flowers to come: perhaps more beautiful than this one, perhaps larger, brighter, and of a greater scent? Or do you celebrate that one event, that moment, as no other, unique unto itself: *perfect and immeasurable*?

You are that flower.

You are all the seed and the bloom... the wisdom and the coded intelligence of life.

You are the nurturing consciousness that is gifted with the opportunity to witness that moment of perfection.

Simply because it can be.

Simply because it is.

And you are every bit a part of it, as you are a future, a past, and an unknowable quantum of light emerging.

PART THREE

GAIA

Introduction by Pepper Lewis

Dear readers,

For over fifteen years, it has been my privilege to be the recipient of channeled wisdom from Gaia, the sentience of our planet, and I am grateful for the opportunity to share it here with you. There is a wisdom in channeling that I have not found in any other study or exercise. Meditation is sometimes described as listening to God/all that is, and prayer has likewise been described as speaking with God/the Universe. If that is so, then channeling is both.

Although I have been lonely at times, I have never felt alone when Spirit speaks through me. The words have always been warm, compassionate, and direct, the information supportive and encouraging. Perhaps I should also say that it has always been up to me to decide what direction my life would take, with Spirit (or Gaia) as my copilot.

Things are changing very quickly now, and as soon as we begin to feel that we have mastered the present moment or the current challenge, the next one reveals itself. Although channeling does not remove obstacles from our path, it does offer us a more profound understanding of what is taking place and a way to navigate through turmoil with the least possible effort.

Gaia tells us that 2010 is a year of both personal and planetary discovery, a year to think with the heart and feel with the mind. She has also described the year as one of "reversals," meaning that we may change our mind, our direction, or our fortune. "Be the observer first and the participant second. Be the witness, not the judge. Be the voice of reason when it does not exist elsewhere, and above all, make certain that your voice is heard by your own heart first, so that your truth will be communicated as you wish it to be."

I leave it to Gaia to introduce her sentience to you in her own unique way and to invite you to experience the Earth, its kingdoms and elements, in a different way than you may have contemplated before now.

With deep respect for your journey,

—*Pepper Lewis*

From Gaia

Esteemed readers,

I am the sentience of this planet, and its soul and purpose is also my own. A sentience is like a thought that is also a feeling that is also a knowing; it is an expression of this all the time, without exception. I am aware of your individual thoughts even when I do not address you individually. I am aware of your feelings about the Earth and about your life. My awareness does not allow me to change personal or planetary circumstances, but it does allow me to investigate and invite new possibilities, especially when they are also of interest to you.

This planet is your home for the time being, and you may shape it to your liking. As a unique representative of the human kingdom, you are free to explore the dimensions and the thin veils that bind them, making it appear that there is but one dimension and one reality. Together, we can explore multiple dimensions and realities where *there* is also *here*. Although it is not my intention to shorten your journey or your ability to explore every experience fully, you may discover that you can easily and creatively be more selective.

Have you ever taken apart a garment so it could be made to fit better? Even while it was apart, it was still yours and you could imagine how it would fit when the work was complete. Well, 2010 will be a little like that. At first it will seem as if someone has handed you an ill-fitting garment and told you to make the best of it. Then it will occur to you that with a little creativity and a little skill, it could be made much better. And even if you do not feel that you have the skills to make the necessary changes, you will find that you can locate and join with others who can assist you.

Perhaps you will allow me to be a member of your extended family that you call on in moments both small and large. Perhaps you will notice that I am present in what you are and what you do, in what you think, and even in what you eat. I am both resource and resourceful. I am the mother of all that is Earthly, as well as a trusted companion and friend.

TWENTY-NINE

INSIGHTS

I greet you, I welcome you to this moment, I welcome you to your life. It is time now to come into the beingness that is life. Life is experience, life is in the discovery of the moment, and life continues to unfold whether or not you pay attention to your life or to life in general. Therefore, the purpose of this planet Earth, celestial body Earth, is also to continue to unfold life. As life unfolds, it is important to uphold it. Life must be maintained as sacred so that it will continue to reveal itself, and when life becomes less sacred, that balance must be restored. This is the time to do so. It is the time now to *restore*, to *rebalance*, to *rededicate*. It is a time, then, not of endings but of beginnings.

So it is time to rededicate the Earth, to rededicate your life and your heart. It is also time to reignite a passion, to rediscover the self, to begin by recognizing the sacredness of each moment. With that recognition, all things unfold in a lighter capacity. Without that recognition, life carries a little more density, a little more burden, a little more responsibility. Know that life always wishes to be rebalanced, to shrug off that burden, and when that rolls off it tumbles, and there it gathers a force of its own. Whether that force is light or density, it tumbles and moves and accumulates until it lands somewhere!

Now that accumulation of energy has landed, there it is now where all can see it. Now it is of monumental proportion. Now there are none left that can turn away and say, "I did not see that." You may say you did not see it coming, but you can no longer say, "I do not see it. I do not acknowledge it."

The *it*—what it is—we will discuss as well. All that has taken place thus far, in terms of the world as you see it now, is that it is beginning to shrug off that which does not serve, that which is no longer appropriate, that which cannot sustain itself. In order for the Earth to continue to maintain itself now, it must be able to sustain itself. In order for you to maintain your health, you must also be able to sustain yourself in this world. In other words, it falls to you to inhale and exhale appropriately for you; it falls to you to maintain adequately the hydration of your body, the proper maintenance of yourselves, your digestion, your nutrition; it is up to you to sustain your body and therefore engage life appropriately.

And so the Earth, my body, must do the same. It must also maintain and sustain in order to encourage life to further life. That is the balance that now is being restored. To say that it has fallen out of balance can be acknowledged, but the difficulty with humanity is that the moment we acknowledge that something is out of balance, out comes the finger that points, "It is your fault," "It is your doing," "It is this," "It is that administration," "It is that presidency," "It is that resource," "It is that abuse," and so on. And yet I tell you that life falls in and out of balance all the time. Your day comes in and out of balance. There is a natural flow, a progression in upliftment and sustainability, when you are more in balance than not, and yet the balance itself is an ebb and flow. It is a force that pulls away from itself and attracts. Attraction and pulling away, that is the consistency of it.

The time period from 2009 to 2012 and beyond is to restore and reignite, to rebalance, to bring forward, to ascertain all the new resources and the new thoughts, the new paradigm of the Earth and of humanity. So all will have to deal with this. As you think about your own concerns, look to see what can be ignited, restored, and discovered. Think to yourself that it is both a beginning and a midpoint in which to do so. So it will not be difficult for you to reach far into the future. It is already here. All that you need is already here or almost here. What is missing is humanity. Simply the acknowledgement to say, "Yes, I choose it. I call it. I welcome it. I work for it. I discover it."

THIRTY

WORLD ECONOMIES AND WEALTH MANAGEMENT

The world's economies are center stage at this time, and perhaps you would all agree that they appear to be somewhat in shambles now, and so they must be restored. It will not happen overnight. Well, it could, but humanity will not allow it to happen overnight. Why? Part of the reason is that humanity has a reference point called the past. Each person has an idea or an ideal of a time when life made sense, when life was appropriate, when life felt as if it was prosperous or creative. That idea is somewhere in the back of the mind of each of you, each structure, each entity. A corporation, as an entity, may have a point in time of that as well—a measure, a scale—just as each individual does.

So the difficulty now is that humanity wishes to restore the economy by putting it back where it was. You say, "Let us go back to that economy, to this president, to that time, to this banking, to that currency." I say to you, that will not happen. It is not appropriate to relive another moment that has already been lived. Instead, it must be re-created, rediscovered, and reignited. There must be the birth of the new from the old, or from that which is now. Until that choice is made, there will continue to be the struggle that you know now—that cycle of being up one day, down the next day. It could be your mood or your currency. But I will tell you that it is your moods that manage your currencies, those numbers that you watch on your televisions. Then those numbers change your moods.

So this measure by which humanity calls the right choice or the right economy must be changed. Humanity says, "Let there be change. We have voted for change," but that is not entirely the case. It has voted for the word *change*. But your life has not yet changed. So you have voted for an ideal. It is yet to be seen whether that ideal will in fact be lived or not.

In this next four-year time period, you will recognize the true meaning of the word *change*. You will then live the word. But not yet, not as immediately as you would like or would hope, and that is not because "they over there" are not willing to change; it is because "you over here" are also not quite ready for the change that is coming.

It is a time period of discovery, of finding peace in what is and in what is not. In terms of the change that will come in the economies, as for the year 2009, there will continue to be the up, the down, and the turnaround.

Also, by the time you read this, there will more than likely be one or two currencies that have fallen or are about to. They could be purchased or absorbed by another world currency. As this happens, the world will then own, to a certain degree, the real estate that goes along with those currencies, and so there is a redistribution of wealth via currency, and you will see that one country can indeed take possession of another without having to go to war. The others will simply surrender.

Currencies will dissolve, others will become more potent, and the entire subject of currency will rise to great prominence. There will be a struggle within the entire banking community for which currency to uplift first, for it will seem that the moment one goes up, another goes down, and the minute there is an improvement in one sector of the world, another will find itself in grave danger.

As some of the world currencies fail, we have said that some will be uplifted, and those that are uplifted will then become more prominent. As you might imagine, those that are largest on the world stage now are those that will be claimed and rise again to great prominence.

Here is how to look at it. The countries that have the most debt, where that debt can be collected or redistributed, those are the currencies that will rise the highest. So here I tell you that it could be the U.S. dollar to rise. I will tell you that the currency of the Red Dragon—what you call China—will rise also, and there will be a rise and a fall in the currency of Japan and the currency that maintains the European markets. For the time being, South America's currency will be ignored.

In the next two years, there will come a reinterpretation of all the systems of value by which your stock markets are interpreted. What you now call your Dow, and all the others as they are lifted and changed, will be exchanged for other systems, for those components that make up the current systems are no longer accurate. And because that inaccuracy will then continue to spread distrust and fear, they will need to be reinvented. And so there will come another measure for investments. There will come the introduction of protections for those investments when the new systems come as well. The ones that will come will seek to bring forward all the world markets. It will not simply be one country's currency that evaluates the market; it will be put forward as a world organization to maintain the value of all of the world's markets and currencies. Even as you read this, there are those that are gathering to bring forward this very subject and how to implement it. So here we speak of a very near future event.

The implementation of the new system will cause a collapse of the older system, but it is not a true collapse. It is more that one system will absorb the other, as when one corporation absorbs the debt of another and simply applies a new logo that looks a little nicer. So it will be the same here, and it will be marketed too. It will be made quite palatable. It will make you feel very snug and secure. You will once again feel that your governments and those that guard your economies are protecting your assets as well as others'.

But for a time, there will be the Band-Aid over the world economies, particularly the North American one. Like it or not, the North American economy is the one the world looks to. It would seem to the rest of the world that if North America can fix its problems and come up with solutions, the rest of the world will follow suit. With that understanding, that is exactly what will take place.

In the near future, you will see attrition of some resources, control of others, protection of still others, and the unfolding of new programs to sustain and raise the world economies from where they are now.

The economies of the world must sustain themselves, just as we have said earlier that you too must sustain yourself. Some will do this well, and some will not. You will see certain conditions upon the planet come into prominence. Certain countries will rise to great prominence briefly, like a solar flare from the sun that is emitted and bursts forth to be noticed and recognized but for a moment and then forgotten.

This will be true of almost every country, not only the United States, because the world is hungry for a solution and will take almost any idea that comes with the right promise, even if there are many, many strings attached—most of which are invisible, at least for the time being. And that is the pitfall with the time that comes. The caution is that you cannot see the strings that are attached. They say to you that they are transparent. I say to you that they are invisible, and there is a difference.

So pay attention to the world that you choose now. Choose the world that you wish to live in. If you do this, you will see that your consciousness will begin to direct the very philosophy that you choose for yourself in life. This is the reason for the coming forward now. As the world economies change, exchange themselves, those on the forefront of these will change as well.

THIRTY-ONE

THE HERO'S PATH AND THE NEW LEADERSHIP

Here is something very important. Choose your personal heroes that you have on the world stage now. Follow them with your thoughts, with your consciousness. See where they go and if your consciousness wishes to follow that. See if they are truly your heroes or if they are simply momentarily on a stage, dressed in a certain way to appeal to you, and then decide for yourself. Perhaps you will discover that you are a hero.

The path you are on, that you have chosen, that has brought you to the Earth now, is called a heroic path. Perhaps you did not know that. The journey you have long been on, the difficulties you have undertaken, the subjects you have considered, is called the hero's path, or the heroic journey, and it is called that purposefully. So perhaps you will discover the hero within. Perhaps you will see that those upon the world stage are less than heroic, and perhaps you will find within your own communities, within yourself, the true heroes. And, in discovering them, uplifting them, perhaps you will give them voice—perhaps you will give them purpose.

Perhaps that is the passion that will be ignited. The heart stands outside itself now, and the heart must also be uplifted; it must be repositioned in its place of glory. Place your heart where it truly belongs. Your heart is intelligent and compassionate. It is only knowledge. And for those who allow it, the heart will even see. Let it see then. Let it discover the next world, this world that now unfolds, consciously. Let the heart be the director. To say that the heart is the director is not the same as to say, "Feel the moment and let the heart go with the feelings." Rather, it is letting the heart be the director of all of the organs of the body, of all of the systems of thought that occupy you. It is the heart that directs the purpose of your life. It manages the energy of the body. It directs how much of that flow you will participate in actively and directly, and so it is the heart, the organ, that must be uplifted—but truly so—to the center of your being. And to do so will then uplift your economies as well. Again, the economies of the world here cannot simply continue as they are now.

It is a time of exceptions to rules, and it is a time of exceptions to those who rule. So you will see that there are many on the world stage that will not last now. The writing is on the wall or in the small print, depending upon how you see it. And even those that rise to power will fall from grace very quickly, at times, to be replaced by others. It will be difficult, for a while, to memorize who is the captain of order.

I tell you also, the new economies will bring to the world new leaders. But the leaders that come to the economies are not necessarily those that are part of your government. Those in charge of the world governments and those who are leaders are not the same. A leader and an elected official are not the same. Leadership is a skill that comes to those who live in support of something greater than themselves. Leadership qualities can be developed within elected officials. Some of them develop these qualities after they have left office. Perhaps you have noticed that.

While they are in office, power becomes their master—the desire to be powerful in a way that affects the world becomes masterfully needed, and so they do not become true leaders until they have learned to control how they respond to power. And so if you wish to look for who your true leaders are, when it comes to true questions of power, of decision, of change, look to see if the decisions, the agenda, are based on leadership for all, or even for some, or on power for the many. That will be how to discern for yourself.

There will come new leaders with great leadership qualities from the private sectors, and they will recognize that in order to remain leaders, they cannot—they will not—enter the halls of government, because the halls of government, for the most part, are corrupt now. They are corrupt beyond corruption. Even those that are newly elected and those who hail the changes they will bring, they still walk the same corrupted hallways as the others. They walk the same foundation, they breathe the same air, and, to a certain degree, they cannot escape that corruption. In essence, they have been elected as leaders of a free world, and yet they are captive within an office that threatens their ability to lead a free world.

And so many of your true leaders will emerge from a private sector. These are the ones to celebrate, to assist. Look to your own communities. Look to what is just in your life, to leadership within you—uplift that, note it. And when you find those true leaders, notice them, what they do, how they do it. When someone says to them how great they are and that they should run for office, hope that they do not.

THIRTY-TWO

THE NEXT BEST THING

You might ask: what is the next resource, the next investment? It is what is within the oceans, what they carry. This is the best next investment. There are particles released now into the oceans from the melting of the glaciers that have been held there for many thousands of years. Many of these not only have a restorative effect upon the oceans, they will be measurable, and so humanity will say: "If it is that all of these particles can restore the oceans, what can they do for the Earth? What can they do for humanity's health?" I say to you now, for those who seek it, add to your diets, to your nutrition, all that comes of a nutritive quality from the oceans—not simply the sea salt and such but what you can add of the kelp, of all of the seaweeds, and of other particularized minerals that come from the oceans. That will jump-start your body's ability to regenerate and to recover your health much more quickly than others.

Another aspect is desalination. It is another important resource for the world now, for it will *seem* that there is much less water to be had. It is not so, but it will be seen that way. Also, the melting polar ice caps are revealing resources that were unattainable before. It was simply too difficult to reach them, to mine them. And so now the great race is on. A millennium ago, there was the race to discover other worlds, other continents, and now the race comes for the resources, to claim them, to own them, and to manage them. And so the United States, the great bear that is Russia, and other smaller countries will vie for these resources.

I tell you that all is well with the world, in spite of all appearances. There are enough resources to feed the hungry in the world. There is enough money to be distributed to the world, enough to restore the world's economies. There are resources beyond your fossil fuels and your oils and gases and such, and these will begin to step forward this year as well, for in order to jump-start the economies, there must be the next resource. There is the next technology. There is the next undertaking.

THIRTY-THREE

CONSOLIDATING WASTE

In order to embrace our next topic, you must hold yourselves not responsible but accountable. You must hold yourselves in a state that acknowledges to some degree that you are human, you are divine, and you are conscious and aware and make choices. At the same time, there must be an admission ... not of guilt but a simple admission that not all things are known or understood, not all choices that are made are the best choices.

With that acknowledgment comes the ability to choose wisely, to choose again, to restructure, and to restore.

This is needed so that we can confront the subject of waste because it is a great issue for this world right now. So it is important that we address this subject in order to know how to consolidate waste, to put agents upon it that will assist in breaking it down, in dissolving it.

The problem itself must be managed, and it must be done first upon this world so that what you take, borrow, or mine eventually from the other worlds will be done in a manner to bring justice and balance to that world, that planet, that celestial body. But you have to do it here beforehand. Otherwise solutions will be further distanced from the problems. In order for humanity to discover what and how to do with the waste that has accumulated, you all must first acknowledge to yourselves that you have been wasteful. It is one thing to say, "I have purchased a little too much, much more than I needed, and that is wasteful." It is another to do something about it.

Before going into the topic of physical waste on your planet, let's talk about waste on a personal level. You see, in this world, there are many kinds of waste, not only the one that accumulates in the pits that are dug, in the fires burned, and all of the ways that humanity finds of decomposing waste. There is waste in thought also, waste in the mind and waste in the heart.

In their own way, these are more dense than the physical problem of waste. This also is garbage, and the rest of 2009 should be a time to rebalance within, in the family unit and in our relations with others. In that awareness and acknowledgment, you will find the abundance of answers—resources and solutions.

Know that when one aspect of the world becomes imbalanced, when one aspect of yourself becomes unstable, it has a cascading effect. As we mentioned before, the ball begins to tumble and roll, accumulate momentum. It cannot be ignored. And in some ways, you will all be forced to see it. And waste is one of these balls.

When you are no longer able to purchase as you have been, or you no longer purchase what you did before, the ball will grow. The accumulation of products, those that remain unsold, becomes waste. They are no longer products just sitting in a warehouse; they are waste that has been created. So in order to find a solution to this—as quickly as possible—it is best to simply pause for a moment and notice where the waste is in your life.

The purpose here is not to find fault. It is not that Gaia comes forward and says, "Clean out your closets and garages," though that is not a bad idea. But it is to say, simply notice where there is waste of any kind in your life. Also think about the waste of your energy. There is a part of your being that is always engaged in creativity, who wishes to use every bit of its energy in a creative stance, for a creative solution.

Free your mind of uncreative thoughts—discard them or write them down, and then set them aside, freeing your mind to contemplate other creative thoughts that are not wasteful or wasted. As you acknowledge this within, very quickly you will begin to see how your outer life begins to change and restructure itself around these thoughts. Either you will have a free section within which to think creatively again at a time when it is most needed, or you will find a solution that until now you could not sort out. You will free yourself to communicate with others creatively and openly. You will see that some of the subjects that you have been considering in your life or have been fearful of addressing will rise to the surface simply so that you can notice them. I tell you, notice them. Notice whether they are useful or wasteful or wasted and if you can give them life and purpose. Where there is no purpose, set them aside or dissolve them appropriately.

Now imagine if a great part of humanity begins to do this, then the subject of waste and waste management becomes very prominent. People will ask: What do we do with nuclear waste? What do we do with industrial waste? What do we do with consumer waste? People are hungry for solutions; humanity will come forward and ask these questions.

One of the thoughts that will emerge is that we simply will ship it out to space. The thought will be, "We will condense it as much as we can, smash it up, and compress it down. There is plenty of space out there." That is one of the solutions that will bring consequences. I tell you, what is safe to decompose here is not necessarily safe to decompose elsewhere.

If this idea is explored, the waste will be placed in a certain pocket of space that seems stable, that looks as if it cannot be seen from Earth, just sitting there in nothingness. I tell you that the process of that decomposition will make that part of space unstable. That great idea, this wasted thought, will come crashing down onto Earth.

So as I say look to your minds and your hearts for what is waste and wasteful, there is great purpose in doing this. Perhaps you will be saving your own backyards.

This is only one of the ideas that will be considered. Another one is to store a greater and greater amount of waste, farther and farther down into the Earth. You now have the ability to excavate more quickly and deeper down into the Earth than ever before. Some will want to create storage facilities to push the waste down into the Earth. If this is done, this will heat the surface of the Earth much more. The decomposition process as the waste is compressed deeper into the Earth will accelerate the planet's warming cycle, and it will trigger other Earth effects based upon a warming mantle.

If this is done, there will be greater earthquakes. This is not difficult to see. Not much science is required in order to see that this could very quickly take place. These are some of the ideas that are being considered even now.

The difficulty with not managing waste correctly and with not correcting this soon is that the concept of lack has already been put forward—lack of currency, lack of oil, lack of resources, and so on. That concept is alive and well, whether or not you think about it. The seeds have already been planted and spread throughout the entire world.

Although before people would say that lack is a Third World problem, now that issue is spreading to the entire world. Managing waste becomes important because humanity will wish to have more space, will need more places to grow food for a hungry world that is still expanding. So in order to have more areas to grow more food, you will need to decide what to do with the waste, all the by-products of this.

Another of the immature solutions—for they are only that—that will come forward is to bury and compress more of the waste and to cover that with very healthy topsoils and all other ingredients that are known to support and sustain life and then simply begin to grow food there again. You will see what happens. It will become increasingly difficult to see where food has been grown or manufactured, to see what countries it has been imported from.

You will see that there is certified food and that there is certified organic food. These are not the same. One that is certified by a government or an authority will simply be one that is granted permission under certain circumstances. And so there will be many other divisions of what you would term organic food, natural food, certified food, imported food, and it will become increasingly difficulty for you to know what each terms means for your health. The subject of your waste, food that is grown, and your well-being must be addressed together, not separately.

So as the world continues to evolve and tries to decide what to do with its waste, certain countries will do more than others. Some will admit to certain toxicity levels, and others will not.

This will also create jobs for those who are willing to take more hazardous employment in the dismantling of some of which has been created. Some jobs will require certain qualities that not everyone has because the job will be dangerous as they will be dealing with hazardous and dangerous waste, for example. So first, it will be broken down by more toxic means, and of course if you use toxicity means to break down toxicity, the poison is still present. So this misunderstanding of the way of doing things will need to be evaluated as well.

To those who devote themselves to waste management now, I can tell you that there is a great career ahead of you but also great challenges—and some of these will be moral challenges.

The world will continue to approach this subject, discovering other ways of managing waste and empowering individual efforts to better do so.

Look for communities that suffer economically to become very creative in how they can manifest more abundance for themselves—how they can generate for the needs of their community. As these ideas are implemented, some will be better than others, and some will become models, ideals for other cities to follow and implement as well.

What you now consider to be simple recycling programs will be almost obsolete compared to what is possible. These ideas will come forward quickly. From these original thoughts will come the birth of a new industry that will bring about new careers and create new economies.

THIRTY-FOUR

WELLNESS AND FEAR

At this time, humanity is under stress. The more humanity continues to be under stress, the less you will be able to manage the nutrition within your bodies. The more susceptible you become to illness, discomfort, and disease.

In certain areas of the world, where thoughts and environments are more toxic, it is easy to imagine that the physical bodies of the people living in these areas will also become more distressed.

Their bodies will not oxidize food properly and engineer all that comes into their bodies as well. Even if they do consume nutritious components, many of these nutrients will be used very quickly by the body—absorbed by the bloodstream but not sufficiently to refuel the thoughts, brain, or heart.

You will see more difficulties of the brain. You will see more brain tumors ... more malignant brain tumors. And you will see that there are more distresses of the heart and arteries that do not operate normally.

People must restore and replenish the idea of health. The idea of wellness must come first. So it becomes more important than ever to think creatively—which is not the same as thinking positive thoughts. A positive thought simply has a direction. A positive thought goes this way, and a negative thought goes that way. Neither is an empowered thought. A creative thought blossoms, it creates itself. A creative thought, an original thought, births itself. With creative thought comes health, wellness of the body, wellness of the mind. When you draw a creative thought, you also draw a creative breath so that the diaphragm changes, restructuring itself.

When you think a creative thought, the mind is so engaged that it involves the entire brain, which changes the chemistry of the body, the flow within the meridians, the structure. Your entire posture changes.

That brings me to talk about fear. Certainly you have seen people with fear and have been yourself in a position of fear. Fear is closed. Fear does not allow you to breathe. Fear is caught in the chest and cannot even replenish itself before the out-breath comes.

In a time of great change, fear comes for many as well. Fear in: Do I go forward, or do I go backward? Do I go back to what I was doing before, or do I go forward to what is the unknown? That fear, that uncertainty, brings its own lack, which first affects your health and well-being. Lack of well-being is not illness; it is simply a distress of the moment. It means that you are not in your truth. You are alive, but you are not alive and well. In order to reengage your consciousness and your creativity, you must de-stress first the self or the moment at least. This is a fancy way of saying that *you must clear your mind of the fog that occupies it in the moment of fear.*

With fear spreading as rampantly as it does, the unwellness of the body will bring about its own demise for some. Poor air quality will also cause lung ailments because there is more ash content in the air now than before. The world has had so many fires. Also, a different kind of dust has been released now because of the quaking of the Earth. This dust has been compressed in the Earth for thousands of years. All this affects the lungs.

But mainly distress and stress are dangerous to your health, wellness, and ability to be creative to bring forth the solutions that are already here. If you see a fog of fear, you will not recognize the solution of the light that is behind it.

So choose life; it is important that you call it that: I choose life. Say "I have an affinity for life. I have an affinity for the divine breath, an affinity to create life and the solutions of life itself." As you do this, you will see the structure of your being change. Your body will redistribute its energy more appropriately. The breath and the diaphragm change and restructure themselves. The pulse and the beat of the heart will change and balance, and then you will begin to notice that you have a different hunger for nutritious food.

THIRTY-FIVE

NEW EDGE MEDICINE

Private investments will also be a large part of the near future. Private financing will fund what we will term edge medicine, which is even beyond what you would now term the frontiers of science. It is that which is beyond medicine and science, or at the very least, it is the two coming together. If there is a frontier beyond where they have merged, that is what we will call the edge. It is the edge and beyond the edge. And because it will come from private financing, it will be allowed and even encouraged. Particularly as illness continues to grow to epidemic proportions, particularly in certain sectors, the race will be on to bring forward this medicine.

This edge medicine will be able to talk to the brain and communicate with the liver to restore it. It will able to communicate with the spleen and inform it that it must have more red blood cells or more white blood cells in order to recover balance. We are speaking of intelligence here, and so edge medicine can also be called intelligent medicine.

Certain compounds will come from nature also—some from the plant kingdom, others from the minerals of the oceans, and others from the metals that will be involved in restructuring all this. There will be new medicine, and there will be the old allopathic medicine. And these will be side by side for a time.

The newer economies will also have private insurance companies endorsed by those who have invested funds into these private studies that will show great results. Many people will be able to enter these programs. At first the insurance will be offered only to those who are either greatly courageous or wealthy, but then it will be offered to others as well. And so the two types of medicines will exist side by side. It began in 2009 but will not find its realization in 2009.

You talk about edge medicine. Does this include the stem cell?

That is not edge medicine—that is already *known* medicine. Yet there will be reaches of that science in which certain cells will be discovered. This will connect with edge medicine, but it is even beyond this. The science behind the stem cell is needed to get to the next science.

Does edge medicine include energy medicine? Will the consciousness of the body be acknowledged?

To some degree, it will. The energy of the body and how to use that energy, how to exist with and beyond that energy, how to draw energy into the body, in the same way one consumes water. This will be acknowledged as well.

Do not believe that what I have said is so far-fetched indeed. All that I bring to you is already present and rises to a certain prominence in 2009, so it becomes recognized and uplifted even if it is not made manifest completely in this year.

Will edge medicine help autistic children?

They will not be the first candidates to try this medicine. The primary candidates are the soldiers returning from war—they will be the first to be rehabilitated. They already took a chance on life, so they are so much more willing to take a chance to recover.

Eventually the brain will be given an instruction: regenerate an arm or a leg. It will be able to take the instructions and begin to grow cells to restructure the body.

Later will come assistance for those that are of an autistic nature and all the other offsprings. It will take those who resuscitate themselves, those who heal and regenerate themselves from this—in other words, those who have emerged from that state—they are the ones who will create a solution for those who remain in that state. They will know the journey that they made, and so they will be able to create the pathways needed for others. That will come from a type of medicine, but not exactly the type that was described here.

THIRTY-SIX

THE KINGDOMS

Many of you are wondering if the different kingdoms are aware of lack of water and oil or if they are aware of global warming. In fact, the other kingdoms and elements are not really separate from you; they only seem so. Likewise, humanity's apparent problems are not real, but they do seem imperatively so. Woven into and between every kingdom, element, atom, and particle is awareness that evolution is quickening everything at an unforeseeable pace. Fear of the unknown is not as prevalent within the other kingdoms, so you would not find a similar response to the changes that are taking place as those you might find within most of humanity. Of course, the other kingdoms do not gather around the nightly news, nor do they awaken to the morning's dismal dose, which explains at least in part where humanity is placing its awareness.

The kingdoms and the elements are what they are, know what they know, and relate to life as life relates to them, in reciprocity. Reciprocity is the state or condition that grants equal advantage and mutual exchange to all things and relationships. It may not seem to humanity that you also exist in this condition, but it will. This state of unrealized consciousness silently expresses that all is well and broadcasts this message vibrationally throughout all the kingdoms of nature, including the human kingdom. This peaceful expression supersedes any knowledge of global warming or concern for the environment. It recognizes every change as the next expression or experience. Viewed from outside this experience, it might appear that the other kingdoms are oblivious to what is taking place, but that is not the case.

To be specific, there is not a lack in oil, water, or other resources. There is a redistribution of wealth and assets of every kind, including oil, water, and many more. There are also new and vital resources waiting to be discovered—and more than likely exploited, at least for a time. The other kingdoms understand lack, but only on a momentary basis, as an expression of the *now* moment. As an example, a common squirrel will not stash away more nuts (resources) this winter than last.

The next several years will be creative for some and accursed by others. As always, there is a choice. It is a time to remake yourself and your world. Polarity is bending now. Positive and negative are no longer at opposite ends of the scale. They are next to one another, alongside dark and light. If you wish to stop long enough to visit a place called "lack," then do so, but if at all possible see that you do not dwell there, as there are many other more wonderful places to explore.

The physical Earth, and my sentience that directs it, both needs and desires restructuring if it means to transcend the dimension that would otherwise destroy it. Humanity will soon follow suit and claim its rightful place as a divine race rather than a forgotten one. Although restructuring takes place at a submolecular level and a nonlinear pace, its results are observable at an experiential level.

As I did long ago, I now bring you a direct, but not so subtle, experience of each kingdom. Each offers its own collective voice, and you would do well to receive it as such as long as you do not perceive it as separate from the sentience that understands itself as whole. To do so would be an injustice to both the message and the messenger. Your mind and your heart are unique and distinct from one another, yet the soul nurtures both as one.

The Plant Kingdom Speaks

Our words and our voices are collective. We seem to you so different from one another because a tree is not a flower, and a flower is not a vegetable. This is true, but we are not as different as you might imagine, and you are not as different from one another either. We choose to honor that which unites us and to celebrate that which makes us unique. Humanity would do well to follow this example, and it is our hope that you will.

It is with a little apprehension that we share these words with you because we do not wish to be perceived as critical of another kingdom. We are as actors in a supporting role, we are here to benefit, assist, and sustain the other kingdoms. We are a natural resource, a sentient extension of the physical planet. That is to say, we are self-aware as individual species and as the collective consciousness you call the plant kingdom. Our awareness allows us to be in communication with many other species, and we are vibrationally attuned to the needs of the other kingdoms because this is aligned with our purpose.

SUPPORTING ALL LIFE ON PHYSICAL EARTH

Our purpose is to support the physical Earth and all life upon and within it. We understand ourselves to be a renewable resource, and we delight in the many and varied uses by which we are employed. For instance, we are pleased to offer ourselves medicinally when appropriate and necessary. Healing is of great interest to us, and many of our plant species have as yet undiscovered properties that we are eager to share with you. Interestingly, some of these properties would be considered controversial and most likely illegal within your cultures due to their narcotic influence. Still, these plants—or rather the fibers within them—would be of great benefit to you because they are self-healing, meaning that they are aware of the purpose for which they are being introduced into a system or body. This kind of intelligence would make the healing process more quick and effective because communication between two or more sentient systems would take place and would not delay or dull the process of healing as is common today.

Toxic shock happens when there is an inability to send or receive healing communication messages by one or more aspects of physical existence. An impasse is created when the body believes an invasion of grand proportion is about to descend upon the very system it has sworn to defend. When one kingdom is unable to recognize another as a mirror of its own perfection, then difficulty, disaster, and death often follow. This is true at all levels of experience: the physical, the superphysical, and the supraphysical. Our experience has proven this over time, as has our interaction with all levels of matter and nonmatter within each kingdom and each Earth element.

FEEDING ALL WHO HUNGER FOR PLANTS AND VEGETABLES

We are guided and influenced as individual species to respond in one or more ways. We are influenced, for instance, to feed all who hunger for what we offer. To that end, we allow ourselves to ingest the chemical formulations that are offered into our soil and water, although we would prefer to reject these.

We do not possess individual will. That is to say, we cannot as individual plants choose to reject what we are fed, and we are destined to allow nature to take its course. However, we trust in the longevity, rejuvenation, and regeneration of this sentient planet (our home) to sustain and guide us through uncertain times such as these.

We do not mind that we are consumed or otherwise utilized to benefit humanity and the other kingdoms. This allows us to serve the purpose for which we were created, grown. We would prefer to be consumed completely so there would be less waste. In fact, if this were the case, there would be little or no waste because most species have been organically designed to benefit the Earth in many ways that are still misunderstood. It has been our experience that the current mind-sets among those who study us slow our evolution and yours more than the pernicious environmental quality that surrounds all present-day kingdoms.

Our kingdom—which consists of plants, trees, seeds, fruits, vegetables, roots, leaves, fronds, stems, flowers, and all of the by-products of these, including those that are released into the air, water, and soil and consumed by fire—composed these words that now reach you. This same collective voice acknowledges our kinship to you and to the other kingdoms. We thrive when you do, and our conscious awareness transcends when yours does. The most evolved within our species are those whose purpose is fully understood and implemented. There is little differentiation as to whether we are serving to cleanse the liver of carcinogenic toxins or delivering a fragrant sense of well-being to a stunned or lonely heart. Our simple desire is to be in communion with all life at a cellular transformative level.

We exist only in the present moment. We are fully aware and sentient of our permanence in the present moment, but we have no awareness of the future as you do. A cabbage, for instance, is aware of its roots and every nuance of the soil that supports it. It is aware of its growth and its purpose, its neighbors in the garden, and all the elements that support it. It is aware that its purpose serves a greater good. Upon maturity it experiences a transformation as it is taken from the garden and introduced into a different environment, and it experiences yet another transformation when it is consumed and experienced by another kingdom. All of these experiences take place as cellular sentience; they belong to the species and to the kingdom.

We are aware that you are concerned with your future, yet we wonder: if that is the case, why are you not concerned with the present? It is one of the many aspects about humanity that we do not understand. For our part, we will continue to offer ourselves as we do, fully, completely, and in unconditional service to that which we call Great Wonder. We are content to be what we are.

The Animal Kingdom Speaks

We offer these words in one of your commonly used languages. We speak in many tongues and make many sounds, but our most common method of communication is what you would call body language. You also speak this language more often than you think but often prefer to use words to communicate even when your eyes and your body contradict this. In our language there is no subtle misconception, no attempt to deceive. When we are hungry, our intentions are well known, and even under cover of brush or darkness, our energy emits a frequency that speaks what words could not say.

COMMUNICATION AT AN ENERGETIC LEVEL

Many of us are predators, and many humans are too. But our methods of hunting and our attempts to feed our hungry families differ in many important ways. For instance, our body language and our vibration might say the following: "I am a mother, and I must feed my hungry children. I honor your life force and the choice you have made to place yourself before me. By taking your life, I further honor you as I will place your life force into my own body and that of my young."

Does every species within our kingdom offer these thoughts prior to taking a life? No, because not all species are self-aware. Still, within what you call animal instinct, there is a communication that exists at an energetic level. Humanity does not like to think of itself as predatory, and it is likely that you prefer to call yourself a consumer.

We are considered the closest to the human kingdom in brain capacity and in development. We understand that you consider some of our primate species a distant relative of the human race. We hope you will not take offense if we do not always think this is a compliment. Those who volunteer themselves into your experimental care do so by choice, and those who make attempts at communicating with you via symbolic language do the same. You believe that science is investigating nature, but of necessity nature must turn a wary eye toward science. Volunteers from every species participate in your experiments and live among you as you see fit. It is a collaborative effort on both our parts, though many times what is learned seems to be of little benefit or significance to either of us.

Our history is as varied as yours. Many of us are native to this planet, but some species were born elsewhere, genetically speaking. We find it interesting (and fortunate) that your predatory instincts find little interest in species that have origins elsewhere. It appears that what is not in your cellular memory holds little or no interest to you, so in some ways our paths are parallel, never intersecting. We are interested in the present and the future but have no interest in reconstructing our past. This is not because we are only interested in the survival of our individual species but because we understand that perfection has brought us to this moment and will carry us beyond it. Development within the animal kingdom takes place at a different level of experience than for humans. We understand this and do not begrudge the many paths humanity takes in its effort to understand who and what it is while expanding in awareness.

LACK OF CONCERN FOR ANIMALS

What concerns us most as a kingdom? The longevity of certain species, the departure of some of our companions, the encroaching of humanity in habitats that are precious and already few, and the lack of awareness with which our game animals are seized and thought of as wholesale commodities.

Are we advocating that you become vegetarians in order to save our numbers? No, we understand your needs because we understand our own, but a severe lack of concern for us may soon become a concern for yourselves. When one species or kingdom turns upon another, the result is often disastrous for both. Already there are viruses, infections, and other anomalies within the game animals you consider to be part of your food supply. This is not simply due to poor handling but also to a true breakdown of communication between and within species. True respect and communication supports interspecies and intraspecies wellness, whereas lack of respect and poor communication breed illness, which, when ignored or unattended, complicates issues further. We place no blame; we simply offer this topic for your consideration, as the opportunity to speak our truth has presented itself.

SPECIES ARE DEBATING TO WITHDRAW

We know that you are concerned about our ocean-dwelling friends, and with good reason. Their goodwill toward humanity has not been met with much kindness in return. You marvel at the oceans, their depth, beauty, and color, and the myriad life-forms found within it, but you take its permanence for granted, and that permanence may change. Levels of awareness within each species allow them to make collective choices within that awareness.

The continued presence of certain species, even those that number in the thousands, is not assured. Historic precedence has little ground to stand upon, for never before have so many adjustments been necessary within so many species. There is confusion within even the most sentient of species, and the choice to withdraw en masse is being debated at an energetic level.

This choice could severely affect humanity and the rest of the Earth kingdoms. What if some of the integral cells of your body departed all at once? Your body would be forced to re-create itself, if indeed that were possible. Cells that are normally used for one function would have to immediately be deployed elsewhere, and a state of emergency would exist in your body. The same would be true of the oceans if several species depart. Collectively, we hope that this is not the case. It is our further hope that humanity's continued pattern of awakening will elicit the care and concern that this subject deserves, for alone we can do nothing.

We have more in common with you than your daily experience acknowledges. Although our present-day circumstances may be very different, our future is more alike than not. We are both dependent upon the Earth for our survival, but beyond that we are dependent upon one another if we are to evolve in consciousness and awareness. You believe that your development as a species is tied to the chronology of the stars and what they will bring, but do not forget that the

Earth viewed from space also appears as a star. If you wish to learn, gain, grow, and expand based upon what you learn from others, would you not wish for something to share or demonstrate in return?

The Mineral Kingdom Speaks

We are the oldest kingdom of record. It is true that we are an Earth kingdom, but we are much more than that as well. The diversity of our resources encompasses a vast part of the Universe. Many of you are more comfortable living in one geographic area over another. Although you may believe that it is the breathtaking coastline, the open plains, or the forest canopy that draws you there, it is more likely that the composition of what is underneath the ground (the support) is what keeps you there.

The Earth is a composite of universal particles of density that created the planet's physical mass. This composite is not distributed evenly but in uniquely and strategically placed energetic vortices. These seeming anomalies give the Earth the diversity with which to enrich itself. They also serve as passive/active, receptive/conductive force fields that channel universal energy to everything that exists upon and within the Earth. The radiation from the sun maximizes these energies, intensifying, lessening, and stimulating their effect in order to promote accelerated growth of all that is within the Earth's influence. These force fields of energy can influence an increase or decrease in the population of any species. They also influence how you relate to your environment because, as a sentient species, you track these energies everywhere you go. The difference between you feeling at home in one crowded city over another may therefore lie in what is underneath you, the substrate material of the Earth or the content and influence of the mineral kingdom.

ALIGNING WITH THE MINERAL KINGDOM FOR A SMOOTH TRANSITION

Our influence on other kingdoms will soon be taking center stage. Each cosmic age ushers in shifts and changes. Just as humanity is experiencing an awakening of sorts, global warming and other environmental phenomena are awakening a purposeful call within the mineral kingdom to increase the flow of energy our kingdom receives from the core of the Earth. This stimulation affects the entire kingdom, but most specifically the crystalline threads that weave specific energetic patterns throughout the globe. It is no surprise that quartz movements govern your watches and timepieces and that organic and artificial silicon power your computers. As the twenty-first century continues to evolve, one age will close and another will begin. Although these transitions are natural occurrences, how harsh or smooth they are upon humanity somewhat depends on how aligned humanity becomes in relation to both its physical and nonphysical environments.

The mineral kingdom relates to humanity in both physical and nonphysical ways. Our kingdoms are joined, and one is never far from the other. Human bodies contain minerals that are also relative to the Earth; even the levels that support balance and well-being are in ratio with that of the Earth. It must be noted that as the Earth continues to have its resources depleted, humanity will as well. If the Earth falls out of balance, humanity will do the same. Evidence of this is already in your midst, so it is likely that these words will come as no surprise. If you wish to strengthen your bodies, it is advisable to supplement your diets with minerals. Wouldn't it also make sense to supplement the Earth's reserves rather than deplete them?

This is one of the reasons that the human kingdom finds such attraction in crystals of every kind, magnitude, color, and shape. At deep levels of consciousness you are aware that this is the energy of creation. Your participation with this energy acknowledges your desire to be in balance and well-being in heart and soul, in physical and nonphysical ways. Each species within the mineral kingdom attracts a very specific form of energy that it then ensouls. This amplifies the healing and nurturing properties of the energy and personalizes them somewhat. This personalization makes them more or less attractive to you according to need and desire.

Rocks, crystals, gemstones, and precious metals all play a large part in your life. Why are you more interested in yellow gold than white gold, for instance? Or less interested in copper than platinum? It is not based entirely on financial or aesthetic value as you might imagine, although heredity and culture certainly influence your societies. Your attraction is based upon polarity and soul origin more than any other criteria, and it is your body's duty as an extension of your soul to make you as comfortable here as possible. The mineral kingdom influences and assists you from within and without. Its healing aspect is its nature, and its nature is to heal.

PARTNERING WITH THE MINERAL KINGDOM

Crystalline energy has been used to heal and power the planet before. As an idea, it is not novel, though its approach certainly can be. Humanity is beginning to understand just how many ways quartz can be used. Expanding upon these theories, you will soon come upon other ways to channel, rather than harness, energy and healing from the minerals. What is the difference? One method partners the kingdoms; the other places them at odds.

Humanity is still at odds with itself over many issues that it must resolve; the crystals and the energy they will reveal wait patiently until the time is right. Crystalline energy will not allow itself to be used in the fashioning of weapons. This has already proven to be detrimental to all aspects of the Earth. We will lend our efforts to technology but not to weaponry. This has already been tested and found to be true. A mountain hurries not in creating its summit because it knows its crowning is assured; no other is waiting to take its place. The mineral kingdom was the first, and it will one day be the last, but that time will yet reveal itself beyond the now.

It is obvious that the mineral kingdom is the most dense or solid of all, but the properties that govern and direct it are also the subtlest. Humanity's growth has also been subtle in comparison to that of life on other worlds, but that will soon change. Assisted by its partner kingdoms, all humanity will shift into places of higher awareness. It is the desire of the mineral kingdom to make your transition as smooth as possible. We hope you will continue to welcome the assistance we offer you from within, without, and beneath. We will continue to make ourselves available to you until instructed to do otherwise by wisdom and intelligence beyond our own.

THIRTY-SEVEN

GAIA RETURNS

Special Information About Flowers and Domestic Animals

FLOWERS

Flowers were once among the more advanced and aware species upon the Earth. Their vibration is one of the highest in the plant kingdom. It may surprise you to know that some varieties were even the teachers of the first generations of Lemurians. These very potent and intelligent varieties reminded early humans that they were to be the stewards of the Earth. They spoke of the importance of cultivating one's garden. Can you remember? The flowers and plants with the highest vibration are those that are descended from these conscious varieties. They, above all others, understand humanity, its needs, and its journey.

Although earlier we said that plants *restore*, here we will say that flowers *replenish*. This means to say that they nourish, make well, and refuel the inner passion for life. This is why certain perfumes and fragrances have always been so highly prized. The Lemurians, your earliest conscious-capable ancestors, had a very highly developed sense of smell, thanks to the gifts they received from their giant flower teachers, which were in some instances over six feet in diameter. Early Lemurians, careless in their attachment to their physical bodies, became easily dissociated from their physical environments.

The flower teachers taught them to breathe in such a way as to replenish the soul's ability to remain as Spirit in a physical vehicle. The flower teachers were also responsible for assisting in the creation and development of physical lungs.

The true history of these flower beings has fallen into mythology and lore as so many marvelous, but extinct, experiences often do. Here we will simply say that what today passes for whimsical and childlike fairy energy was once a very powerful, yet innocent, elemental wisdom.

DOMESTIC ANIMALS

Many of you believe that domestic animals—pets—can heal their owners and/or absorb so much negativity or illness as to make them sick, and thereby shorten their own lives. I say that this is true, but it is not as common an occurrence as many would believe. The animal kingdom is wild first and domestic second. The human kingdom is domestic first and wild second.

Domestic animals are a small subset of an undomesticated family; they are not simply descendants of wild ancestors. Almost any individual animal can become domestic, but not every species can be domesticated. The difference lies within the subset itself, which can be loosely compared to a soul family.

It is also interesting to note that there is a difference between a domestic animal and a pet, just as there is a difference between a game animal and one raised for human consumption, even if they are the same species. A domestic animal companion can redirect or deflect energy that would otherwise make its human companion sick. It is not healing as you currently understand it, but the result is similar. Animals are highly attuned to frequencies, and they are able to differentiate between them. Discordant energies are disturbingly audible to them, and they often find that it is in their own best interest to cleanse their immediate environment of these whenever possible. Dogs are sometimes able to do this with their bark, by replacing a disruptive frequency or energy with one that is more to their liking. The next time you see a dog barking at seemingly nothing, take note that there may be an appropriate purpose in their activity. Likewise, a cat may lunge at what appears to be nothing at all, although it is quite certain that whatever it pounced upon has dissolved.

Relating to the activity just mentioned, domestic animals could also deflect destructive energies from their owners before they have been absorbed into the aura or matrix of that individual. They are able to lead the energy elsewhere and hopefully replace it with a more balanced alternative. The closer an owner is to his animal companion, the easier and quicker the task. Animals who are allowed to sleep near their owner can do this more easily. A constant or terminal illness is more difficult to treat. Whether or not an animal companion is able to heal its human counterpart depends upon the bond they share, as well as how compatible they are for another. Energy must find a resonance or an *attraction* that it can attach to in order to draw out the poison, as it were. If an animal becomes overly attached to the poison—such as cancer—it may not be able to separate itself from it for long enough to restore its own harmony. Owners are often unaware of the gifts that their animal companions carry or the sacrifices they make.

And is the same true of plants? Yes, but not exactly. A plant has a different existence and offers a different kind of companionship. A houseplant or tree inhales, exhales, pauses, and then begins the next similar cycle. Because these cycles are constant, you would not be able to observe even the slightest nuance that a change has taken place, but within every pause is a moment of oneness, unity. The pause is the restorative cycle, and everything within the plant's field of influence is refreshed. The same is true of outdoor plants and trees, which is why most people find that they are literally restored when they place themselves in nature. Hugging a tree may not be appealing for everyone, but settling yourself close by is enough to draw many benefits.

THIRTY-EIGHT

THE ASCENSION PROCESS

During this transition, you as Gaia have to consider on one hand the beings living on Earth, the duality of it all, and at the same time your own ascension process. From my understanding, a planet has transited before and groups of people have ascended before, but they've never both transitioned at the same time. We are writing our own history, and all the Universe is watching.

How do you feel about all this process from the perspective of your essence?

My sentience anticipates change hundreds and even thousands of years before that change takes place, so there is no surprise in the process. There is an understanding that all things are always and in all ways evolving, and my sentience takes comfort in this. If, beforehand, individuals could see the vast and far-reaching strides that their hardships would accomplish in the long term, they would perhaps feel differently about them. I have the benefit of being aware all of the time. My awareness does not begin and end with each lifetime as it does where humanity is concerned. This will not always be the case, but it is true enough for now.

The process itself is like a midwife and a mother. There are moments of excruciating joy, and here and there a lament crosses my brow as I bid adieu to a beloved species in order to welcome another. The Earth is part of a very unique family of planets, each one purposeful and important in its own way.

I share this adventure with them even as they have shared their adventures with me. I am assisted and guided by their knowledge and wisdom in much the same way that I am able to assist and guide those who are less aware of the process here—only the scale of knowing is different.

THIRTY-NINE

DUALITY

I understand that in the third dimension we have a very dense duality, one that gives us the illusion of linear time. We only focus on one point, and that is our reality, which prevents us from seeing other probabilities that exist. I feel that it is like a roller-coaster ride: we never see in advance what is on the other side; we don't see the drop. It is both exciting and scary. Even if it is very scary, when it is finished we want to go back on the ride. Once we are on the other side, we don't really care about how scary it was; and when we are on this side, we don't really remember who we are, so we get scared again.

Is there progress in the process? Because the purpose is to get out of duality, how can we accelerate this process?

As you know by now, duality is an illusion that humanity does not quite understand yet. From your perspective, the third dimension appears dual in nature, because the Earth is represented by two poles, two genders, etc. But there is a third expression, hence a third dimension. It is the light/dark, fear/compassion, God/not-God *node* that exists at the center of all thoughts and things. This reconciliation of duality is what humanity is, and it is also what it does, at least for the time being. Fear does not exist when mortality does not exist. Do you see?

Progress does not come from maneuvering one's way through a series of lives steeped in duality. Duality is something that people emerge from as they arrive at the center, or heart, of their life or perhaps a reality that has become obsolete. That is one of the wonderful bonuses of this life compared to others: the reality upon which the current duality was based has ended for the most part. This is why you see so many systems and structures falling apart.

Acceleration is a movement toward the center. It is a choice that requires courage and determination. Although it is available to all, many will not choose it because its benefits cannot be confirmed ahead of time. It requires a leap of faith, and a grand one at that. For this reason, the fainthearted and the younger souls wait and watch, for a season, a lifetime, or many lifetimes. Accelerated times are not a guarantee of acceleration in the individual. This concept is misunderstood.

Thought is what creates the next dimension. For the most part, even-numbered dimensions are mental realms that produce thoughts, which in turn create realities, schemas, and worlds. As the third dimension becomes overly dense and begins to break up, thoughts of creating another dimension in which to express oneself emerge from the mind of all that is. The immensity of this mind is difficult to fathom, as is its creative ability. Nonetheless, every detail is accounted for, and a place is found for every particle that exists. The fourth dimension is the bridge between the third and the fifth. Humanity can assist the process by placing its awareness on what you call the fourth and the fifth dimensions, regardless of what is taking place on the third ... a daunting task.

FORTY

THE GRAND EXPERIMENT

I think what makes this experience so unique in the Universe is that Earth has been seeded with genetic material from thousands and thousands of planets. That would mean there is a lot riding on this experiment, not just for us but for all those who have participated. For all these beings and planets who donated their material, the shift will surely have a profound effect on their world. On one hand, they have participated in the experiment and are allowed to watch it live but not participate directly in it.

How do they influence our journey, and is that why we can have such highs and lows on this planet?

The highs and lows are a direct effect of one's core beliefs regarding the meaning of life, and in particular human life on Earth. Until humanity discovers (and believes) the truth about its genetic heredity, we cannot accurately measure or describe the effects of the Grand Experiment. You will pardon the expression, but the result of an experiment often depends upon which laboratory rat tells the tale. Do you see? Whose history and DNA do you have and how much of it—do you know? At what point in time (or outside of time) was it inserted? What were you like before then, better or worse? Are you sure? You see, if you cannot be certain who or what you were in your last life or in-between lives, you cannot yet know the outcome of the Grand Experiment with any certainty.

How and when will you reconcile this? In order to see a truly larger picture and view human existence with a new perspective, humanity will need to set aside almost all its beliefs regarding itself, its history, the planet, and even God. The holy books that have become extensions of a God that is still unfamiliar will need to be replaced with a larger, more cosmic view of this and other worlds. This planet has many histories, and some are more accurate than others. The retelling of a tale, even one that is well told, does not make it expansive or inclusive enough to reflect humanity's true origins.

How does the Internet fit into the future? From what I am seeing, the Internet is already playing a great role in enabling us to find inspiring stories and community projects, in connecting people and helping each other, instead of being stuck with the distorted news that we are shown on television.

The Internet is a tool that seems infinite in its reach, but it is not. The ability to make available volumes of information on demand is a welcome addition to the otherwise stale alternatives, but it too will be replaced by something that is more interactive, more real.

Holographic computers are already on the horizon, as are interactive television/computer/personal management/health maintenance devices that monitor and enhance life. This is not as far off as you imagine, and it will take the world by storm, particularly because the expense will be well within reach of the average household. Of course, there are some drawbacks of significant proportion. Because of necessity, this will be a computer-like device that never sleeps—a robotic entity of sorts—and this may take a little getting used to. Still, it is your future and the answer to the demands of a busy world.

FORTY-ONE

THE AUTO INDUSTRY

The auto industry, which is important for economies everywhere in the world, seems to be having immense difficulties. Is something different on the horizon for that industry?

This form of transportation has become rather arcane, and as seen from afar by those who uphold humanity as a creative and evolutionary species it seems an insult to human ingenuity. But until humanity tires of it and conceives of a more popular idea that suits the individual at large, it will remain in place. Contrary to popular thought, the oil-rich nations and corporations are not what prevent a transition to another model; *it is humanity itself that believes that an automobile is a defining attribute of individuality and status*. It is an old belief but one that is still strong and represents a significant portion of the Earth's population. Humanity has not yet conceived how to build without cranes for heavy lifting or other giant-scale machinery to fulfill its demands. It has not yet created the replacement for trucks that haul garbage to landfills or for diesel trucks and coal-based trains.

The new model will be introduced when the current one is almost exhausted. It is moving in that direction very quickly. That is one of the reasons why there is such little concern for how or when the current accumulation of debt will be repaid. It cannot and will not be repaid, like the queen bee in the beehive, which lives for many seasons in service to those who have installed her as their monarch. The queen is protected at all costs, but in the meantime those who serve also feed off the queen a little at a time. Eventually the queen exhausts its usefulness and a replacement must be found.

The present system must first be proven obsolete. It will not be allowed to die easily or generously. It will be slain, and its head (or the symbol that represents it) will be mocked. Its weaknesses have already been exposed, as have the riches of those who have lavished upon themselves its largesse. By the time Obama introduced his rescue plan, it was already too late, but he had to do it to make it seem that something could be done, because so many people depend on the car industry for their livelihood. Now, under the restorative efforts of the newly elected, the benefits of the new model will be introduced. The advantages of the new model will be obvious and will include something for almost everyone, from those in the highest echelons to those in most need of charity. The new model will do away with the accumulated debts of the old, and it will allow almost everyone the same advantage. It cannot be said how soon it will come about, simply *that it will* or that it *already has*, depending upon how it is viewed.

Please remember that *who* you are and *what* you do to earn a living is not the same. Even if finances fail, life will provide an option here and a possibility there. You can never lose *everything*—only what you have today. You did not arrive with your present resources, and you will not depart with them. Therefore, they are only for your use in the here and now. The same applies to those whom you would leave your treasures to and to those who assume it is theirs by rights of inheritance. The same is true for everyone. If you have lost a fortune in this system, perhaps you will increase your wealth in the next economic model. Therefore, pay close attention to its nuances when it is first introduced. Those who believe in the benefits of a new reality will find them sooner than those who do not.

FORTY-TWO

2010 AND BEYOND

What does the immediate future hold?

In the immediate future, there will be a renewal of interest in all things spiritual, established or otherwise. Established religions will be favored, at least in the beginning, because in the current moment there is an increased need for stability and security wherever and however it can be found. Established religions will seize this opportunity to increase their membership and advance their cause. Most will enjoy at least a temporary gain. Some will even advertise with their cause by hiring agencies to make their words appear more golden. Those who are experts in their field will indeed gild the words as if they were heaven-sent.

Newer religions and offshoots of established ones will have their own say, as will more cultured and open-ended secular movements, including those that unfold themselves from within the branches of the New Age. Expect the advent of more mystery schools, modalities, and modern traditions. There is value in that which empowers the individual to author one's own life. Be aware of that which scorns the beliefs of others or drags through the mud the good name of those who have earned it. Trust the voice of Spirit as it unveils itself from within and displays itself throughout your life. Spirit is not constrained by religion nor constrained by the good opinion of others or lack thereof. It is resplendent in the form and the formless, and you will recognize it as it speaks the language of universal law.

Your spiritual awakening occurred at the dawn of time, which was long before this life. There is a subsequent new dawn, or awakening, in each life, which is unique to the purposes of that life. This life is no exception, as by your own acknowledgment an awakening has already taken place. The latest round of world events is just that—a virtual carousel that goes around and around the same track. It only appears different than the last time because the frailties (not failures) of human nature make it seem so.

Many more things could be said about your future in the years to come. I have shared some of it with you in these pages. As for 2010, I invite you only to do one thing, and that is to participate in life differently, to behold yourself and your world in a previously unrehearsed way.

Ask yourself this: *to what degree am I participating in my life wholeheartedly and without reservation?* In answer to this question, assign it a number that, after careful thought, you have settled on. Choose another number (percentage) and decide how much you are willing to risk in order to achieve a higher level of participation in life. Decide that a wisdom far more than what you are aware of in this moment has the ability to bring about this result, without any specific action on your part.

Choose 2010 as the year in which life becomes your partner, without exception. Make this your truth so that no matter when you revisit this moment, it will still be your truth, the full measure of your being.

FORTY-THREE

CONCLUSION

As you have welcomed my words today and those of my kingdoms that I have offered to you, I wish to say that soon you will welcome a new kingdom: *a generation of humans that is poised to become the first to be considered genetically divine*. These beings were born beginning in 2007 and will reach maturity in twenty-two years. Their agenda will be explicitly peaceful and their nature expansively creative. They will be engineers and architects, scientists and healers. They will be interested in healing the present and creating the future. You will exclaim and take note of the color of their eyes that will be decidedly violet. Later, you will take note of their deeds, which will positively influence your own and confirm the life that you have been aspiring to live.

I leave you with these words:

There is but one world, and it contains many peoples.

There is but one world race, and it is multicultured in appearance.

There is but one measure of prosperity, and its root is layered in compassion.

There is but one Earthly resource, and it is called Man.

There is but one truth, and it is visible within all that is invisible.

There is but one thought which alone precipitates itself, and it is called Mind.

There is but one thing that alone precedes itself, and it is called Light.

There is but one origin of humanity and one solution for it, which is to restore itself and suffer not the effects of the wheel of birth and rebirth.

These above words are *protected*, meaning that they have always existed in one form or another. In desperate moments they have been one breath away from extinction, but even the breath, which is holy in origin, contains two parts and is dual in nature. Therefore, even when hope surrenders, fate intervenes—the opposite being true as well. Although these words have been revered and kept secret (protected) by brotherhoods and initiates of certain means, they have also at times been offered to laymen (men who follow the rule of law first and higher law second) to solve and to save as the case may be. Those who have tried in error over countless eons of time to interpret the words by ones and by twos have called them a riddle and even a curse. But for those who dare, they are words to live by, for in them and by them the future of humanity also lives, but which future that will be and what it will look like is still to be seen.

Look for good news, not in the day's headlines but within yourself. Look for the good within you and put that to work for you, for everyone else, for the planet, and for life itself. This tool is lifetimes old and will always serve you. Offer something good to others and to the world every day. To *offer* is to extend; it is a presentation or extension of quality. Even as large-scale events unfold, remember that life is lived in the smaller, more personal moments. You are more affected by the breath of a butterfly you have never met than by the heated breath of world debate. Breathe deeply. Breathe because there is life force in the breath, and this same life force has the brilliance of a thousand suns.

Those who promote global headlines are well trained to coax a response in their readership. Your response, although not trained or rehearsed, is often collective. You can train yourself to respond through your higher awareness rather than through the more obvious human collective. You will not be less than human or less compassionate by elevating the vibration of your response. Rather than expressing with the sigh of exhalation, respond with a deep inhalation and you will see an almost immediate difference in how body and mind relate to one another and to the collective. Spirit will see to that. You can share the world with others without sharing the same worldview.

I can no longer offer you dress rehearsals in which you improve your costume but not your part, but I remain committed to the evolution of a conscious awareness that will spark your true nature now and always. I am always in your debt, heartfully present and hopelessly underfoot.

Until we meet again,
Gaia

ABOUT THE CONTRIBUTORS

LEE CARROLL
Channel to Kryon

After graduating with a business and economics degree from California Western University, Carroll started a technical audio business in San Diego that flourished for thirty years. Timidly, he presented the first Kryon writings to the metaphysical community in Del Mar, California, and the rest is history—with a total of twelve metaphysical books released in a ten-year span. There are now almost one million Kryon and Indigo books in print in twenty-three languages worldwide. The foreign editions represent Spanish, French, German, Chinese, Hebrew, Danish, Italian, Greek, Korean, Hungarian, Bulgarian, Russian, Lithuanian, Latvian, Japanese, Dutch, Finnish, Slovene, Estonian, Indonesian, Portuguese, Romanian, and Turkish. Carroll is the coauthor of *The Indigo Children*, *An Indigo Celebration*, and *The Indigo Children Ten Years Later* and a contributor to *The Great Shift*. In 1995, Lee was asked to present Kryon at the United Nations (UN) in New York City before a UN-chartered group known as the Society for Enlightenment and Transformation (SEAT). The meeting was so well accepted that Carroll and Kryon were invited back five more times—in 1996, 1998, 2005, 2006, and 2007! These meetings are held upstairs in the working areas of the UN building, not far from the General Assembly. Only delegates to the UN and guests of the society may attend.

Carroll lives in San Diego with his wife, Patricia. Visit his Web site for more information at: *www.kryon.com*.

PEPPER LEWIS

Channel to Gaia

Pepper Lewis is a natural intuitive, a gifted channel, and a recognized writer, speaker, and teacher of metaphysics. The distinctive channeled messages brought forth by Pepper have become favorites of readers all over the world. Most popular are the featured articles authored by the sentience of our planet, Mother Earth, affectionately known as Gaia. These messages frequently appear in a variety of publications including the *Sedona Journal of Emergence*. They are also a favorite with many Web sites and news groups. Pepper is frequently featured on radio and Internet broadcasts including *The Great Shift* with Rev. Fred Sterling. She is the founder of the Peaceful Planet, an organization dedicated to relating to our environment and the world around us in a way that embraces and projects balance, integrity, peace, and harmony. The Peaceful Planet offers inspirational products and services designed to empower, assist, and educate. Seminars, lectures, and workshops are ongoing as time allows. Inquiries regarding scheduling an event in your area are welcome.

For more information about Pepper Lewis, visit her Web site: *www.thepeacefulplanet.com*.

PATRICIA CORI
Channel to the Sirian High Council

Patricia Cori, a native of the San Francisco Bay Area, has been immersed in the New Age movement since its inception there in the early 1970s. She has utilized her clairvoyant abilities in healing and support work throughout her life. As channel for the Speakers of the Sirian High Council, ascended extraterrestrials holding resonance at the sixth dimension, she has scribed *The Sirian Revelations*, a trilogy of teachings intended for the awakening of humankind at this pivotal moment in Earth's evolution. She is also a contributor to *The Great Shift.* She is well known on the international lecture circuit, offering courses, seminars, and workshops in the United States, Canada, and abroad on a vast range of topics, which reflects her broad knowledge of alternative methodology in healing and her conscious awareness of the higher knowledge. She offers training in DNA activation and a certification program for DNA facilitators, as directed by the healing teams of the Sirian High Council. She lives in Rome and can be reached via her Web site: *www.sirianrevelations.net*.

MARTINE VALLÉE

Publisher, author, and director of this series

The interest in all that is spiritual started very early in Martine Vallée's life. At eighteen, two books changed her life: *Life and Teachings of the Masters of the Far East* by Baird Thomas Spalding and *Life After Life* by Raymond Moody. Since then, she always believed in the power of words to transform and heal the soul. Since 1994, through *Ariane Publications* and with her brother Marc Vallée, she has been publishing spiritual books for the French community around the world. Her purpose is to give her readership as many tools as possible to enable them to better navigate these times of great change. She made the commitment toward humanity to explore the path of knowledge and share it. She considers her readership a very big part of her spiritual family.

Martine is grateful to all the wonderful authors who dedicate their lives to inspire and transform the world by bringing back the real nature of consciousness. For the next part of her life, she will also be working toward many humanitarian projects. One of her first projects through her foundation, Passion for Compassion, is to help and assist women in the Congo who are victims of sexual terrorism. All her projects will be chosen in the same manner that her books are: through guidance from her heart and passion for humanity. This foundation will also be a grand experiment in compassion, and she plans to involve her readership. We will see how a group of ten thousand dedicated people will be able to influence events and change the world one heart at a time. It will be launched officially on January 1, 2010, in French and English. She strongly believes that the combination of love, compassion, and pure intention creates a force by itself, a force that is strongly represented with the return of the divine feminine. This energy is in every human being, and it is our responsibility to put it forward. Martine lives in Montreal and shares her time between her family, her friends, and her work.

Write to her at: martine@passioncompassion.org or martinevallee@qc.aira.com. Please visit her website too: *www.passioncompassion.org*.

TO OUR READERS

Weiser Books, an imprint of Red Wheel/Weiser, publishes books across the entire spectrum of occult and esoteric subjects. Our mission is to publish quality books that will make a difference in people's lives without advocating any one particular path or field of study. We value the integrity, originality, and depth of knowledge of our authors.

Our readers are our most important resource, and we appreciate your input, suggestions, and ideas about what you would like to see published. Please feel free to contact us, to request our latest book catalog, or to be added to our mailing list.

Red Wheel/Weiser, LLC
500 Third Street, Suite 230
San Francisco, CA 94107
www.redwheelweiser.com